Library
St. Joseph's College
Patchogue, N.Y. 11772

NATIONAL ISSUES IN EDUCATION

ELEMENTARY AND SECONDARY EDUCATION ACT

Edited by
John F. Jennings
Director
Center on National Education Policy

Published by
Phi Delta Kappa International
Bloomington, Indiana
and
The Institute for Educational Leadership
Washington, D.C.

Cover design by
Victoria Voelker

Library of Congress Catalog Card Number 95-68412
ISBN 0-87367-479-0
Copyright © 1995 by Phi Delta Kappa and
The Institute for Educational Leadership

TABLE OF CONTENTS

Preface v
   by Douglas Bedient and Michael D. Usdan

Introduction vii
   by John F. Jennings

Commentary on the Nature of an Omnibus Bill xiii
   by John F. Jennings

PART I: GENERAL THEMES OF THE ESEA LEGISLATION

**The Improving America's Schools Act:
A New Partnership** 3
   by Marshall S. Smith, Brett W. Scoll, and
   Valena White Plisko

A Nickel on the Dollar 19
   by Richard P. Mills

  **Reinventing Education in the Image of
   the Great Society** 35
    by Bruno V. Manno

PART II: THE CREATION OF THE NEW TITLE I

**Improving America's Schools for Children in
Greatest Need** 55
   by Thomas W. Payzant and Jessica Levin

Making Schools Work for Children in Poverty 77
   by Kati Haycock and David Hornbeck

PART III: OTHER MAJOR PROGRAMS

Professional Development and Education Reform 93
   by Congressman Thomas C. Sawyer

The Chapter 2 Program 105
   by Congressman Steve Gunderson

Beyond Ideology: Educating Language-Minority Children Through the ESEA 109
by Congressman Xavier Becerra

Bilingual Education and the Future of America 119
by Congressman Toby Roth

Impact Aid: Education's Bramble Bush 129
by Senator Claiborne Pell

The 1994 Reauthorization of the Safe and Drug-Free Schools and Communities Act 135
by Senator Christopher J. Dodd

PART IV: SOCIAL ISSUES

The Reauthorization of ESEA 145
by Gary L. Bauer

The Holy War on the "Unholy" Elementary and Secondary Education Act of 1994 159
by John H. Buchanan

PREFACE

Phi Delta Kappa and the Institute for Educational Leadership are pleased to co-publish this fourth volume in our National Issues in Education series. Like the previous volumes in this series, our purpose in *National Issues in Education: Elementary and Secondary Education Act* is to present diverse perspectives on how current major national education issues are addressed in the legislative process of the U.S. Congress.

This final volume in the series examines the prominent elements of the omnibus Improving America's Schools Act, including the reauthorization of the landmark Elementary and Secondary Education Act (ESEA). The authors of these essays not only articulate their own positions and perspectives, but in so doing they also shed new light on policymaking issues and processes.

Our purpose in developing this series of books has been twofold. First, the books serve to illuminate the work of influential players in the development of national legislation that affects education. Second, these books offer important historical perspectives. As the issues themselves become part of our national education history, they reveal their foundations in past policies and practices and set a course for the future.

Elementary and Secondary Education Act brings this four-volume series to a fitting close. The National Issues series began with *The Past Is Prologue*, which examined the transition from the Administration of President Bush to that of President Clinton. The second volume, *Community Service and Student Loans*, looked at the first two major pieces of legislation from the Clinton education agenda. *Goals 2000 and School-to-Work*, the third volume, viewed the cornerstones of the Clinton Administration's school reform strategy. And now, in this final volume, the cycle is completed with an examination of the omnibus reauthorization bill.

Again, we are indebted to John F. (Jack) Jennings for conceiving this series and for serving as its editor. Jack began this work when he was general counsel for education, Committee on Education and Labor, U.S. House of Representatives. Jack retired from that position earlier this year.

We are pleased and grateful that Jack has chosen to continue this important work in his new role as director of the newly established

Center on National Education Policy in Washington, D.C. The center is co-sponsored by Phi Delta Kappa and the Institute for Educational Leadership.

We hope that this publication, like it predecessors, will be used in classrooms across the country, as well as generally among educators and those concerned about education policy. These national education policies help to shape the future of education in our nation. These books, we believe, enrich the general discussion and understanding of how those policies are made.

        Douglas Bedient
        President, Phi Delta Kappa

        Michael D. Usdan
        President, The Institute for
        Educational Leadership

INTRODUCTION
By John F. Jennings

The National Issues in Education series is intended to further the understanding of how education policies are made in Washington and to explain the reasons for such policies. The writers in this volume, like those in the previous three volumes, have generously assisted in fulfilling that purpose.

This book is particularly important at this time because most of the federal programs aiding elementary and secondary education were substantially changed in 1994 in order to make them supportive of state and local reform. Because this federal assistance totals more than $10 billion a year, distributed to nearly every school district in the nation, the effects of these momentous changes will be felt in most schools in the United States during the next few years. These changes are contained in the legislation called Improving America's School Act, the most important component of which is the revision of the landmark Elementary and Secondary Education Act of 1965.

The most recent major effort to reform public elementary and secondary education began in the late 1970s, when certain standardized tests seemed to show that many students were not learning basic subject matter. The reform movement gained momentum in the 1980s as the states increased high school graduation requirements; demanded greater teacher accountability, often by mandating the testing of both students and teachers; and pumped more money into the schools. In the present decade the states have furthered reform by developing higher academic standards for students and by experimenting with charter schools and other innovative practices.

For most of this 20-year period the federal government has stood on the sidelines, watching the spectacle but not daring to plunge into the fray. As a consequence, the education programs supported by federal aid often have not been synchronized with state and local school reform efforts. U.S. Secretary of Education Richard Riley told the nation's governors in August 1993, "In most states and school districts, federal programs such as Chapter 1 have remained outside of, and irrelevant to, the overall reform process." Furthermore, Riley pointed out, if left unchanged, the situation would soon become a major roadblock to change because some states are mounting reforms, such as revised testing and evaluation systems, that run contrary to requirements in federal programs.

In 1989, President Bush began an effort to bring the federal government into school reform by promulgating, with the help of the state governors, the national goals for education and then by submitting several legislative proposals to Congress. Although his Administration was successful in funding the development of national content standards for education, Bush's legislative initiatives to broaden the federal government's involvement in school reform were defeated, mostly because of his support of choice and voucher programs that would aid private schools.

After assuming office in 1993, President Clinton proposed legislation that was similar to Bush's but differed in several significant aspects, in particular by not extending support to private schools. After much congressional debate and several votes on controversial amendments, Clinton was able to sign into law the Goals 2000: Educate America Act of 1994. At last, the federal government had entered the battleground of school reform.

Soon afterward, Clinton signed into law a complementary reform program, the School-to-Work Opportunities Act, which backs up the Goals 2000 bill by providing an alternative way for the states to change high schools and to move students toward achieving the high academic standards proposed in Goals 2000.

Both bills buttress the efforts that the states began on their own in the early 1990s to base their education systems on content and student performance standards. This "standards-based" reform focuses on teaching and learning as the core activity in schools, instead of concentrating on such piecemeal approaches as site-based management or choice programs. The starting point of standards-based reform is agreement on what should be taught and what should be learned. Then the different components of schooling — assessment, teacher training, textbooks, and so on — are aligned with the content and performance agreements in order to make the greatest impact on student achievement. While individual reform measures may help, they will not be fully effective unless, and until, the core functions of teaching and learning are addressed.

The legislative controversies that swirled around the enactment of federal support for standards-based reform are described in the third volume of this National Issues in Education series, *Goals 2000 and School-to-Work*. The background to those bills — namely,

President Bush's proposals and the congressional battles they gave rise to — are set out in the first volume of the series, *The Past Is Prologue*.

This final volume of the series describes the successful effort to bring the large federal aid-to-education programs into accord with the new agreement contained in Goals 2000. That agreement, simply stated, is that the federal government ought to help, instead of hinder, the states in their individual efforts to raise educational standards and to base reform of their elementary and secondary education systems on high standards. Secretary Riley has said that the Goals 2000 bill set out the framework for the federal government's involvement in school reform; the other bills help to fill out that framework. Thus this volume continues the story that began in the first volume with President Bush's proposals and was carried to a successful conclusion in the third volume with President Clinton's initial legislative achievements.

The Clinton Administration used Goals 2000 as a model of how to refashion federal aid. Riley and the Education Department worked to bring most of the major federal programs into alignment with standards-based reform. Therefore, the legislation that the Administration presented to Congress to revise federal aid to education was coherent. All the pieces fitted together. And after considerable debate, the Congress adopted the ideas proposed by the Clinton Administration. Thus in October 1994 the President signed into law the reauthorization of the Elementary and Secondary Education Act and related acts, thereby initiating the most significant changes in the federal aid programs since many of them were created in the mid-1960s. By these means, the federal government not only entered the school reform effort but also changed its major programs to support reform.

This volume will tell the story of how the federal aid programs were updated in order to support higher standards for students and state and local reform based on those standards. In Part I, the writers review the general debate that occurred and the general thrust of the changes. Marshall Smith, the Under Secretary in the U.S. Department of Education, with the aid of Brett Scoll and Valena Plisko, describes the Administration's ideas. Smith is especially well-qualified to do so because he has been promoting the use of standards and systemwide reform since the 1980s. In his Education Department role he has been charged with making the federal programs into a coherent whole. Therefore, he has been instrumental in drafting many of the Administration's legislative proposals.

Next, Richard Mills, the chief state school officer in Vermont, shows how federal programs had been working in a school-reform state and how the revised programs will assist reform efforts in the future. Vermont has been in the lead in raising student achievement standards.

Bruno Manno, now a scholar with the Hudson Institute, was an official in the U.S. Department of Education during the Bush Administration. Manno offers a dissenting view. He disagrees with the overall direction of the federal programs and the recent reforms. He believes that different reforms should be adopted, such as block grants and choice programs involving private schools. Although a minority position in the Congress that passed the Goals 2000, School-to-Work, and ESEA bills, that point of view will certainly carry greater weight in the more conservative Congress now in place.

In Part II, the writers concentrate on the changes that were enacted for the largest of the federal aid programs, Chapter 1, which is now called the Title I program. Thomas Payzant is the Assistant Secretary for Elementary and Secondary Education in the U.S. Department of Education and Jessica Levin is a special assistant in the department. Both played key roles in formulating the Administration's proposals in cooperation with Marshall Smith and in dealing with the Congress as the bill was considered and amended. Both also will be heavily involved in carrying out the changes.

David Hornbeck, now the Philadelphia schools superintendent, has had a long career in education, including serving as the state school superintendent in Maryland and as a principal author of the landmark state school reform plan in Kentucky. Kati Haycock also has held a variety of posts in education and now works on school reform with the American Association of Higher Education. Both were key members of the independent Commission on Chapter 1 that was formed to review the program. That commission issued a report advocating major changes in federal aid, which strongly influenced the Administration's proposal and how the proposal was considered in the House and the Senate.

These writers view the changes in the federal aid programs in the broad context of school reform. Therefore, some parts of their essays seem to dwell more on Goals 2000 than on the ESEA amendments. That emphasis demonstrates how successful the Clinton Administration was in tying these ESEA federal aid programs into the Goals 2000 structure.

In Part III, the next six writers, all members of Congress, describe the changes made in some of the other major programs that were included in the revised Elementary and Secondary Education Act, in addition to Title I. Their essays deal with various issues and give a sense of the variety of policy debates that occur whenever Congress considers a comprehensive bill. However, readers should note that none of the dozens of smaller programs authorized by the legislation is included in these essays. Thus the debates may appear less complex than they actually were.

Representative Thomas Sawyer (D-Ohio) discusses the Eisenhower Act, which provides funds for teacher training and retraining. Representative Steve Gunderson (R-Wis.) describes the changes made to the education block grant program that used to be called Chapter 2. Representatives Xavier Becerra (D-Calif.) and Toby Roth (R-Wis.) provide different views of some of the most controversial changes, those dealing with bilingual education and immigrant programs. Senator Claiborne Pell (D-R.I.) discusses the amendments to the impact aid program; and last, Senator Christopher Dodd (D-Conn.) outlines the modifications to the Drug-Free Schools and Communities Act.

Part IV, the final section of this volume, includes two opposing views of the social amendments that were considered in the debate on ESEA. Gary Bauer, president of the Family Research Council, expresses his reasons for favoring some of these social proposals. Former Representative John Buchanan, then associated with People for the American Way, discusses his reasons for opposing many of these amendments. Both writers are associated with Washington-based organizations that frequently enter into the debate on social issues. Their essays offer a valuable perspective because the social amendments became a large part of the debate on the education bill. Buchanan and Bauer also show how the debate over the Goals 2000 act and its role in school reform spilled over into arguments on social issues.

During the present Congress (1995-96), these social issues are bound to be considered again as various bills make their way through the Washington policy process. The results of these new deliberations may be different than they were in the last Congress, because the current Congress is more conservative. This Congress also may re-open some of the education policy issues that were settled in 1994 in the reauthorization of ESEA and related programs. Regardless of any such changes, it will be useful to understand the reasoning behind the ESEA changes of 1994, which were the most important in the quarter-century of federal aid provided through the Elementary and Secondary Education Act.

COMMENTARY ON THE NATURE OF AN OMNIBUS BILL

By John F. Jennings

In the three previous books in this National Issues in Education series, I have placed a chapter commenting on the various essays at the end of the volume. In so doing, my intention was to encourage readers to first read the various writers' views before reading my own ideas on the political, procedural, and conceptual aspects of policy making. I have decided to depart from that format for this book because of the complexity of the ESEA subject matter. Thus, if readers desire to read the essays before they read my musings, they should skip this chapter, perhaps to return to it later after reading the other essays.

The ESEA bill was an omnibus of legislation. It dealt with dozens of programs and issues; therefore, any book that attempts to describe this legislation must reflect that complexity. The first three volumes in this series of books focused mainly on single issues, such as national service and school-to-work programs. An omnibus bill, by its nature, is complicated; and the policy debates occur at many levels. The essays on ESEA not only discuss the general themes of the major changes but also present the arguments that arose about specific programs within ESEA, each with its own set of related issues. Also debated in the context of the omnibus bill were various extraneous social and cultural amendments.

When readers plunge into these essays, they soon will find themselves being pulled first in one direction and then in another. To keep readers from being sucked under by this maelstrom, it may be helpful to set down a few ideas ahead of the essays. This brief commentary will help readers gain an overall sense of the different views.

Another reason for placing this commentary at the beginning is to carry out the purpose of this book, which is to explain why fundamental changes were needed in federal aid to elementary and secondary education. So many points of view are presented that, after reading these essays, readers might wonder how such diverse opinions could ever be reconciled. Nonetheless, the bill did pass the Congress and was signed by the President. And so a word of explanation may be helpful to clarify the relative importance of the various opinions.

In policy debates, not all views can be reconciled all the time. That is why issues are decided by votes in Congress. In the policy process, especially in legislatures such as the Congress, numerous attempts are made to bring people together through compromise and persuasion, but that is not always possible. On some issues one side has to win.

When the bill that revised the Elementary and Secondary Education Act went to President Clinton, the final vote in the House of Representatives was nearly two to one, 262 to 132. In the Senate it was nearly four to one, 77 to 20. In the end, the support for the revised ESEA was overwhelming, despite all the well-publicized controversy. All the major education organizations supported the final bill, as did the major business groups, the labor unions, and other social and religious associations. The only significant opposition to the bill came from the same conservative organizations that had opposed the Goals 2000 bill and that are generally suspicious of federal aid. These groups had an influence on the more conservative Republicans in the Congress.

President Clinton and his allies in the last Congress were successful, for the most part, in attaining their legislative agenda and greatly changing the way that the federal government aids the schools. But the opponents of Clinton's approach will receive a much more sympathetic reception in the current Congress, because it is much more conservative than the last Congress.

Importance of Federal Aid

The Clinton Administration, its allies and opponents in Congress, and the national organizations knew that the revision of the Elementary and Secondary Education Act and related programs was a major undertaking. The amount of money involved and the scope of influence that the federal programs have on elementary and secondary education are significant. The funds appropriated for the programs in the bill come to more than $10 billion a year, and broadly discretionary uses are permitted.

Most school monies are used for the fundamentals, such as teachers' salaries and the operation and maintenance of school buildings. Federal money, although only about 7% of total school expenditures, is not tied to these basics. Most federal monies are earmarked for "discretionary" spending, which makes these funds very useful for teachers and principals. For example, many schools purchase computers, video discs, and other teaching tools with federal funds because state and local monies for these items are not available. Also, federal funds often are used for the added services that are required to meet the special needs of disadvantaged or disabled children.

Therefore, federal aid is important because it provides dollars that can be spent in ways that best serve children. This flexibility of use is constrained only by the general targeting of the funds, which effectively conveys a national vision of what schools should do. For instance, in the late 1950s a major target was the improvement of mathematics and science education. The National Defense Education Act of 1958 was passed by the Congress in response to the Soviets sending the first satellite into space. In the 1960s schools were able to focus specific attention on the special needs of disadvantaged children because of the passage of the Head Start and Title I programs. In the early 1970s the Education of All Handicapped Children Act led to a vast expansion of opportunities for disabled children.

Thus, when the 103rd Congress turned its attention in 1993-94 to the revision of the Elementary and Secondary Education Act, it knew that it was undertaking a major task that would affect nearly every school district in the country. That legislation and the surrounding debate were complex, and the essays in this book mirror that complexity. Therefore, in order to better understand the controversies that surrounded the bill, it is useful to separate the topics into categories. The first set of issues, which are the most important for education in general, concerned the comprehensive restructuring of federal aid. Essays that deal with these issues are in Part I. A second set of issues focused on the amendments to particular programs; these form Parts II and III. And the third set of issues, in Part IV, concerned social initiatives. These issues gave rise to considerable emotionally charged debate.

Key Issues

A major philosophical shift was realized in the passage of the amended ESEA bill. Previous federal aid tended to be compliance-oriented and focused on specific categories of children. The new ESEA focuses on improving teaching and learning by supporting school reform in the states. These fundamental changes in federal aid are discussed in the essays by Marshall Smith, Brett Scoll, and Valena Plisko; Richard Mills; Bruno Manno; Thomas Payzant and Jessica Levin; and Kati Haycock and David Hornbeck.

As a result of passing this omnibus bill, the federal government will now support education in quite a different way than it did in the past. Most of the major federal programs, including Title I and the Eisenhower program, now will buttress state and local reform efforts that are based on setting higher standards for all students. The philosophical shift is from targeting aid to groups of children identified by their special needs to assisting whole schools to improve learning for all children. Embodied in this approach is an understanding that states and schools will gain a greater degree of flexibility in the ways that federal funds can be used. The federal government is abandoning an approach that relied on ensuring compliance with various rules and regulations.

As schools exercise more freedom to use federal funds to improve teaching and learning, they will be able to combine various federal programs to support schoolwide improvement. The controlling viewpoint is that when agreement is reached on the "ends" to be achieved through schooling, then much greater freedom can be given to teachers and principals on choosing the "means" to those ends. With the new legislation, state and district authorities are urged to change from a compliance orientation to a technical assistance orientation. The federal government also will change its role from rule checker to assistance provider. These changes represent a momentous reform in federal aid to education, the most important since most of the programs were created in the mid-1960s.

The proposed changes brought much debate in Congress, but the earlier passage of Goals 2000 greatly eased the way for the omnibus bill. During consideration of that earlier bill, the use of a standards-based approach to school reform raised intense controversy. The enactment of that bill laid the issue to rest for a majority of the members of Congress. But Goals 2000 also crystallized the controversies; and so the essays on ESEA revisit many of the same arguments, albeit in slightly different ways.

It was important that the amended ESEA reflect the basic Goals 2000 agreement on standards-based reform, because that undergirding philosophy was needed to support the entire reform movement. Goals 2000 contained several million federal dollars and was very useful at the state level in furthering reform, as Vermont State Commissioner Richard Mills points out in his essay. But it did not have the reach of the 10 *billion* dollars of aid that the ESEA programs provide every year to nearly every school district in the country. Thus, when Title I and the other ESEA programs were amended to back up the development of content and student performance standards, thousands of school districts had to take notice and begin to incorporate the standards being developed by their states into their local approaches to school reform.

Kati Haycock and David Hornbeck, in their essay, point out the fundamental changes caused by focusing federal aid on the overall improvement of teaching and learning, rather than on funding separate programs for special groups of children, which often created situations where children were "pulled out" of the regular classroom. Thomas Payzant and Jessica Levin stress the flexibility now built into the altered federal programs, which will allow school-level decisions about integrating programs and how to allocate the federal funds.

Richard Mills' essay is insightful. As a state school superintendent, he agrees that the federal programs will help states in the future in ways that they did not do in the past. Federal aid will be coherent instead of fragmented, and it will reinforce what the states already are starting to do to improve their schools. Mills believes that the federal government came late to the game, but its new direction is good for education. But Mills also points out some serious problems that still have to be faced. For example, through the Individuals with Disabilities Education Act the federal government requires schools to meet the needs of disabled children and mandates the use of certain procedures to ensure that end. But little has been done to bring those children into the larger school reform process. Mills also rightly points out that much of the reform movement is not yet connecting with the ordinary teacher.

Thomas Sawyer makes the same point when he highlights the need for teacher training and retraining. School reform cannot be solely a state or national process; it must change behavior in classrooms if it is to mean anything at all. Finding the funding to train teachers in the new standards is difficult, as readers will see in the debate over folding the Chapter 2 block grant program into the Eisenhower program. Thomas Sawyer supported the Administration's proposal to combine these programs, because that action would lead to greater funding for training. However, Steve Gunderson and others fought to keep that block grant because of its flexibility in the uses of the funds at the local level. This debate illustrates the problem of trying to find extra resources to bring about reform when budgets are tight.

Difficulties with carrying out the omnibus bill reforms remain a concern. But the consensus is clear: The federal government is finally in the game that was started by the states, local school districts, groups of teachers, the business community, and others. For too long the federal government sat on the sidelines and did not support basic restructuring of the schools. The new Elementary and Secondary Education Act has changed that.

Program Issues

A source of confusion in the debate was the plethora of programs that were being amended and the hundreds of changes that were proposed in those programs. The original bill submitted by the Clinton Administration affected several dozen programs, and the final bill that the President signed included nearly twice that many. Those programs touched on such diverse needs as Indian schools, native Hawaiian cultural preservation, and the better coordination of social and medical services for school children. As a result, the debate, especially in the various congressional committees, ranged widely over the policy landscape, depending on which programs were being considered.

Readers can get a taste of this diversity by reading the essays on impact aid by Claiborne Pell, drug education by Christopher Dodd, bilingual education by Xavier Becerra and Toby Roth, teacher training by Thomas Sawyer, and the education block grant program by Steve Gunderson. Those five programs were among the most important ones affected by the bill; but dozens of others were debated, as well as such related issues as the revisions in the National Assessment of Educational Progress. Major pieces of legislation frequently cover a broad range of programs and issues, though only a handful of such questions receive news media attention. Essays on some of the other programs are included in this book to give a flavor of the breadth of the policy debate.

An interesting aspect of the legislative process is that once agreement on the basic structure of a bill is reached, the debate tends to stray into side issues. On the ESEA bill the Clinton Administration and the Congress reached early agreement that federal programs ought to be supportive of standards-based reform in the states. Consequently, there was scant discussion of that issue later in the full House and Senate debates. Instead, those debates went to the different programmatic requirements of the slew of smaller programs in the bill and to the social issues that were appended to the bill.

One source of controversy in the ESEA bill is not highlighted in the essays in this book. That is the fierce fight over the "formula" to distribute the funds for the largest program, Chapter 1 (now relabeled Title I). The omnibus bill contains more than $10 billion in aid to schools, of which the Chapter 1 program had about $7 billion, making that program the most important one in the bill. The method used to distribute that $7 billion is set out in the law as a precise formula using poverty and funding statistics to channel the aid to approximately 14,000 school districts. Whenever the Congress considers an extension of the Chapter 1 program, it usually becomes embroiled in a big dispute over how to divvy up these funds, and so it did during this reauthorization of ESEA. That controversy hung over the bill until the end, when a convoluted compromise was adopted that resulted in shifting some new funding to poorer school districts.

Social Issues

The debates over social-issues amendments are important because they diverted the bill a number of times and almost killed it in both the House and the Senate. Many of those debates revolved around such issues as school prayer, sexuality, immigration, and abortion. The conference report was in danger of defeat in the House because of the resolution regarding the prayer amendment and faced similar peril in the Senate over the same issue, as well as several others. The essays by John Buchanan, Gary Bauer, Toby Roth, and Xavier Becerra help to explain the emotions that those issues stirred.

Since the 1960s, when substantial federal aid was first provided for elementary and secondary education, federal legislative initiatives have engendered debate on broad social and cultural issues. In the late 1960s and early 1970s, many amendments were offered that sought to curtail the court-ordered busing of school children to eliminate racial segregation. In the same period, several amendments were proposed to cut federal funds to colleges and universities that failed to limit student demonstrations. Those debates clearly reflected the social ferment of that time. In the late 1980s, amendments were adopted requiring policies on drug use in schools and colleges; and more recently, federal laws have been changed to require public notice of crimes committed on college campuses with the hope that such publicity will force administrators to ensure a safer education environment.

However, no federal education bill has been the subject of more social-issues amendments than the revision of ESEA. That bill was before the full House of Representatives for debate and amendment for more hours than almost any other bill in that session. This phenomenon reflects the central role that the schools hold in American society. The public and the legislature continue to view schools as vital social instruments. But such exhaustive debate also may demonstrate the current social agitation in American society and how politicians are responding to it and using it for their own purposes.

The essays by Buchanan and Bauer present contrasting views on many of the social-issue amendments, which may be expected because they represented major organizations that figure in debates that occur over a range of social issues. The essays by Roth and Becerra are noteworthy because they discuss the special social tensions that have resulted from the increase in legal and illegal immigration over the last decade.

Interestingly, little debate on social and cultural side issues took place in the congressional committees. Instead, the legislators spent most of their time in committee on issues related to education. In fact, the bills that passed the House and the Senate were basically the same bills that were reported by the committees in terms of the content of the education programs. The major amendments that were added on the Senate and House floors were mostly social-issues provisions on school prayer, sexuality, condoms, and expulsion of students who bring guns into school.

Block Grants and Other Issues

Many of the issues addressed in this book will be revisited by the current Congress. Indeed, as this book goes to press, congressional hearings already are being held that are raising fundamental questions about federal involvement in education. And so it is difficult to foretell the outcomes. It may be useful to look at Representative Gunderson's essay, in which he discusses the virtues of block grants and mentions that they may be the vehicle that the new Congress uses to refashion, yet again, the federal aid programs. Bruno Manno also writes about the value of block grants.

The term "block grant" does not have a precise meaning, but it usually is used in policy discussions to mean the folding together of a number of different federal programs into one grant that is given to the states. The "block" of money can be divided at the discretion of state authorities to fund as many or as few programs as they desire. Often block grants award less money than the former categorical programs. The argument is that block grants costs less to administer than a number of separate categorical grants. Proponents contend that block grants restore power to the states; opponents contend that block grants are merely a device for cutting back on federal aid.

Block grants were considered in the late 1970s when President Richard Nixon tried to undo the programs that were enacted as part of President Lyndon Johnson's Great Society. Nixon succeeded only partially, because the Congress was in Democratic hands. Thus most federal education programs were kept separate, notably Head Start and Title I. In the early 1980s President Ronald Reagan tried again to enact block grants. He had greater success than Nixon did. More than 40 education programs were folded into the Chapter 2 block grant that both

Steve Gunderson and Thomas Sawyer discuss. In 1994 that block grant carried an appropriation of $380 million, compared to an appropriation of some $980 million (using current dollars) for the separate programs back in 1981.

Together, the new Elementary and Secondary Education Act, Goals 2000, and the School-to-Work Act all provide for greater flexibility in the use of federal funds. They all contain provisions for the federal government to waive rules and regulations to permit greater local control over programs. Therefore, the question most likely to be raised is why block grants are needed, given the new flexibility in federal aid.

In addition to the arguments that likely will occur over block grants in this Congress, the Goals 2000 law will be revisited and the premises for standards-based reform also will be questioned anew. This debate will cycle naturally to the revised ESEA. Gary Bauer and Bruno Manno assert that these two laws will lead to greater federal control of education and to outcome-based education, and their views will count for more than they did in the last Congress because the new Congress is more heavily conservative. Thus the conservative members of Congress likely will argue that federal programs should be eliminated or cut back. However, the major U.S. business groups supported both bills and the underlying philosophical shift toward standards-based school reform, as did many of the nation's governors.

Congress has been called a continuous debating society. There never seems to be an end to the discussions or a solution to the policy debates. For the most part, such debate is healthy. It demonstrates the vitality of American society, where solutions are always questioned and new ways of doing things are continually brought before the public for discussion. However, the seemingly endless debates also are frustrating to teachers and administrators, who constantly are buffeted by the winds of political change. Just when they have learned the rules, the politicians change the game.

Regardless of any new congressional debates that revisit ESEA and related acts, standards-based reform is being implemented across the country and will continue to be a key element in changing how schools meet the education needs of students and society. The reason for this persistence is that standards-based reform is principally an initiative of the states. At present, nearly every state is developing or already has developed content and student performance standards.

Most readers will agree that all students should achieve high standards of learning and that the federal government should play a positive role in helping schools ensure that their students succeed and excel.

The federal government also should assist the states and local school districts in school reform, instead of encouraging separate programs that diffuse the energy that teachers and principals might better spend in helping students learn. These purposes drove the ESEA revision.

The revised Elementary and Secondary Education Act is an attempt to update federal aid so that it will assist the states as they go about reforming education based on the concept of high standards for all students. The new law arranges the federal programs into a more coherent format than there has ever been before, and it targets the programs toward the central task of supporting state and local school reform measures. Most observers will agree that these are worthy goals. How well they have been accomplished will be determined in due course.

PART I
GENERAL THEMES OF THE ESEA LEGISLATION

The Improving America's Schools Act: A New Partnership

By Marshall S. Smith, Brett W. Scoll, and Valena White Plisko

Marshall S. Smith is the Under Secretary of the U.S. Department of Education. Prior to accepting this appointment, Mr. Smith was dean of the School of Education at Stanford University. Mr. Smith is a member of the National Academy of Education.

Brett Scoll works in the office of the Under Secretary, where she is a special assistant to Mr. Smith. Val Plisko serves as the division director for planning and evaluation of elementary and secondary education programs in the office of the Under Secretary. Her office was responsible for the latest national assessment of Chapter 1 and other evaluations for reauthorization of the elementary and secondary education programs.

The Clinton Administration's proposal for the 1994 reauthorization of the Elementary and Secondary Education Act (ESEA), formally named the Improving America's Schools Act (IASA), contributed to a significant shift in the federal role in elementary and secondary education.[1] At the same time, it reaffirmed many of the principles on which the ESEA was originally based. This essay sketches the history of ESEA, places ESEA and federal policy in the overall context of education reform, and discusses the Administration's reauthorization proposal and the response of the 103rd Congress.

A Short History

By the mid-1960s, researchers had documented the correlation between school achievement and poverty. Children from low-income families did not achieve as well as children from more affluent families. In addition, poor children in schools with high percentages of poor children did not perform as well as poor children in schools where they had more affluent peers.

President Johnson's Great Society initiative included ground-breaking federal legislation directed especially at enhancing opportunities for low-income Americans.[2] Through Title I of the first ESEA, passed in 1965, the Johnson Administration hoped to advance equality of opportunity by targeting extra resources for supplemental services to low-achieving students in schools with the highest concentrations of children in poverty. In its first year the appropriation for Title I was more than three-quarters of a billion dollars, an extraordinary commitment of resources at that time.

While the bulk of ESEA resources served needy students, additional provisions were designed to improve the overall quality of education. These resources included support for books and other materials, for research and development, and for strengthening state education agencies.

The architects of ESEA believed that the education system was in need of repair, but they also were aware of the significance of the 10th Amendment to the Constitution, which vests the responsibility for education in the hands of the various states. As a consequence, the early ESEA limited the reach of the federal government in administering ESEA programs by emphasizing the role of state and local government and by containing few regulatory requirements.[3]

Over the next decade, dozens of new K-12 education programs were added to the federal agenda. The most important of these programs, such as Title VII, the Bilingual Education Program, and P.L. 94-142, now the Individuals with Disabilities Education Act, supported equality of educational opportunity for new categories of children with special needs. Other programs focused on subject matter related to improving the quality of education, such as arts and foreign languages, or specific areas or groups, including rural education and programs to address school dropout problems.

Federal regulation and oversight also increased, in part as a response to questionable uses of federal funds. Financial audits, especially audits of Title I, carried out by private and public agencies revealed that federal monies were perceived and used in many communities as general aid instead of for the purposes intended by Congress.[4] In addition, evaluations of federal programs, again especially of Title I, showed results that failed to meet expectations for the programs.[5]

The response by Congress in the late 1960s and early 1970s was to focus on fiscal accountability, especially on ensuring that the federal resources were used solely for purposes expressly approved in the laws and regulations. The congressional logic was impeccable: By increasing the chances that the federal dollars were to be spent directly on the intended students, Congress believed it was addressing both the auditing problem and the problem of poor evaluations.

But the strategy had an important side effect. Strict federal regulations and program accountability and separate funding streams for various categorical programs led to the creation of discrete, powerful, and often rigid administrative structures. Requirements that separated and stigmatized students proliferated in response to the demand for fiscal integrity. If children were placed in "pull-out programs" and separated from other students, then the fiscal trail was easy to demonstrate. More important, the administrative requirements affected the curriculum. Many of the student-focused categorical programs concentrated on easily monitored, low-level, basic skills instruction that often resulted in a double deficit of lost regular classroom time and less challenging instruction.[6]

The decline in test scores, "discovered" around 1975, alarmed the nation and stimulated state reform movements focused on "the basics," which included state minimum competency requirements and examinations. This state and local focus on the basics was reinforced by the federal Title I program. One probable long-term consequence of the alignment of basic skills-oriented policies was to contribute to an increase in the test scores of poor and minority students — a trend that reduced the achievement gap between rich and poor and that lasted into the late 1980s.[7] But the "back to basics" movement had its costs, as the overall achievement of the majority of American students, at least as assessed by standardized test scores, showed little improvement.

Stagnant test scores, alarming international comparisons of achievement, and the threat of international economic competition stimulated a new set of reforms in the 1980s, focused on raising the quality of education throughout the nation. The federal *Nation at Risk* report, issued in 1983, sparked and bolstered reform efforts at the state and local level. States established career ladders and tests for teachers, reduced class sizes, and lengthened the school year; districts tried a variety of strategies, including effective schools, site-based management, and in the 1990s, New American Schools. In spite of a great deal of activity at both the state and local level, only a handful of states undertook truly comprehensive and coordinated reforms.

The 1988 reauthorization of ESEA did reflect some of the ideas that had been tried at the state and local levels, though in general the law remained as it had for 23 years. For example, Title I recognized local reforms by emphasizing "advanced" as well as "basic" skills and by introducing a stronger system of outcome accountability. Yet maintenance of federal requirements for standardized, norm-referenced testing at all Title I grade levels actively interfered with some reform efforts.[8]

While federal categorical program legislation remained largely unchanged during the 1980s, the federal government did expand its role in education reform. In 1989, President Bush and the nation's governors held an Education Summit. At this meeting the President and the governors, led by then Arkansas Governor Bill Clinton, endorsed six National Education Goals; and the national Education Goals Panel was formed to monitor the nation's progress toward meeting the goals.

An early focus of the panel was on ways of meeting the goals that called for challenging academic standards. However, there were no clear standards by which to assess the nation's students. This led Congress to create the National Council on Education Standards and Testing (NCEST) to study and make recommendations about the development of national standards.

Although the NCEST report, issued in 1992, recommended voluntary national content and performance standards that would set out what all students should know and be able to do, it also argued that education is primarily a state and local responsibility and emphasized the need for states to develop or adopt their own standards and assessments. The council also recommended that there not be a single national examination; instead, strategies would be created for "equating" state examinations to provide a measure of national progress.[9]

Increasing support for the establishment of challenging standards heightened the need to address major flaws in the design and implementation of ESEA programs. New evaluation, such as the National Assessment of Chapter 1 (Title I), concluded that the program no longer was contributing to reducing the learning gap between disadvantaged students and their more advantaged peers.[10] Evaluations of other programs also indicated serious shortcomings. In the important area of preparing teachers to teach to high standards, ESEA programs were unfocused and too short in duration to produce much of an impact on classroom practice. Most of the professional development programs were relatively brief, were not part of a comprehensive plan, did not reinforce state reforms, and were not sustained.[11] ESEA programs in their current form were unlikely to support changes in teaching and learning that would help children achieve to higher standards, especially as many programs were providing minimal support in basic skill attainment.

As the 1994 reauthorization of ESEA drew near, it became increasingly clear that the federal programs were out of step with the growing reform movement in the states. They were focused on low-level skills and were fragmented. They did not support local and state reforms. And even on their own terms, they often were ineffective.

Passing the Current ESEA

The Clinton Administration entered office in January 1993 eager to apply the lessons of the previous decades to support sweeping change in federal policy. Three generalizations formed the basis for the Goals 2000: Educate America Act proposed in spring 1993.[12] These generalizations do not differ greatly from the generalizations made by organizational theorists who study complex private-sector organizations.[13]

1. Offered the right opportunity, all children can learn to far more challenging academic levels than currently are expected of them. However, students are not likely to achieve to higher levels if they are not challenged and motivated. Simply asking for higher achievement does not suffice for two reasons: First, many teachers have little understanding of and little experience in teaching challenging content and skills in their classrooms. Second, the nation has a history of low expectations and watered down curricula, especially for minority and low-income students. Further, while many teachers generally support the idea of higher standards and a more challenging curriculum for students, they are unclear about what this means, especially as grading and curriculum standards vary across classrooms, schools, school districts, and states. If we are to expect higher achievement for all students, we need challenging common standards to help guide the development of curricula in our schools.

2. Schools cannot sustain reform unless all parts of the school system operate to support reform. Sustained change at the school level often is frustrated and confused by conflicting messages and policies throughout the education system. Federal programs and policies come with a variety of rules and incentives that sometimes conflict with those developed at the state and local levels. Governors may be proponents of different reform goals and strategies than local superintendents; decisions at all levels may be influenced more by political considerations than by thoughtful policy responses. These conflicting messages must be moderated and, if possible, replaced by focused support for enabling students to achieve to high standards. Otherwise, school reform will come and go as it has in the United States for the past 30 years.

3. *Lasting and effective change is more likely to be successful if school staff have ownership and some control over the goals and process of reform.* A substantial body of research indicates the need to enable those closest to students to experiment with a variety of strategies and to decide how best to work with students.[14] The evidence seems clear that resources, flexibility, and decision-making authority should be channeled to the school level.

The Goals 2000: Educate America Act is intended to help states carry out reforms based on these generalizations. The act asks states to undertake a widespread, participatory process to develop challenging content and performance standards and assessments; to set out and implement a comprehensive strategy to focus all elements of the state's education system in support of having all students achieve to the standards; and to channel resources and authority directly to local districts and schools. After the first year, states must allocate at least 90% of their resources from Goals 2000 to districts in order to support planning and implementation of critical reform activities that general education funds cannot support. The intent of the Administration is to build a partnership between the federal, state, and local efforts to improve the quality and equality of the education system while simultaneously respecting state prerogatives.

While the Goals 2000 law was designed to support and encourage state-driven reforms, the rigid structure of other federal K-12 education programs existing in 1993 threatened to impede these efforts. The 1994 reauthorization of the Elementary and Secondary Education Act provided a critical opportunity to revamp other federal education programs to support state and local improvement efforts, instead of frustrating them.

The Department of Education's ESEA proposal was influenced by a variety of sources. The fundamental strategy for the reauthorization was set out in the Clinton Administration elementary/secondary transition team report.[15] The proposal also was affected by the department's internal working groups on the reauthorization and by a large variety of studies and working papers developed by commissions, constituent groups, states, congressional staff, and other stakeholders.[16]

The basic concept was that the Improving America's Schools Act (IASA) should reinforce state and local reforms supported by the Goals

2000 effort. Instead of each ESEA program operating separately, the federal programs should operate in concert to improve opportunities for all students. Federal resources would serve the populations and purposes that the ESEA programs are authorized to serve — such as providing extra assistance for low-achieving students in poor schools or for providing support for teacher training — but the way in which the services were to be provided would encourage ongoing reform efforts by schools and state education agencies. Thus Title I students would be given support to help them learn to the same high *state* standards as other students, rather than having federal rules and standards determine the nature of the Title I program. And professional development efforts would focus on supporting teachers to be able to teach to those state standards.[17]

Within the Administration the planning and writing of the proposal stretched from January to September of 1993. Over time, five principles for the reauthorization emerged to guide the proposal:

1. *High standards for all children.* While research has shown that all children can learn to higher levels than we currently expect, we also know that children in low-income schools served by Title I and the limited-English-proficient children served by Title VII often are held to far lower academic standards than are their peers. In the Administration's proposal, the core ESEA programs were focused on providing support for targeted students to reach challenging state content and performance standards, the *same* standards developed for all students. Congress passed most of these proposals.

2. *Focus on teaching and learning.* Reform efforts are placing a great deal of pressure on teachers to learn new material, new methods of teaching, and new ways to work with other teachers, parents, and the community. Research on effective professional development has found that many such programs share some similar characteristics; in particular, they often involve all or most of the staff in the school and are focused on a long-term, consistent set of goals that reflect the needs of that school.[18] In response to these needs, the Administration proposed aggressive professional development efforts in many of its programs focused on special target populations, such as Title I and Title VII. These proposals were adopted by Congress with few significant changes.

The Administration also proposed the expansion of the Eisenhower Mathematics and Science Professional Development Program to encompass all subject areas and to focus on sustained, intensive, high-quality professional development as described in state and local professional development plans. The Administration's proposal envisioned that teachers would participate in developing local plans that might include teacher networks and other forms of long-term professional development opportunities. The proposal was designed to consolidate Chapter 2 of ESEA and the Eisenhower Math and Science Program into a larger Eisenhower Professional Development Program with a larger funding authorization. Congress accepted the substantive changes for the Eisenhower program but chose to keep Chapter 2 as well.

3. *Provide flexibility to stimulate school-based and district initiative, coupled with responsibility for student performance.* One of the common complaints of local and state education officials is that compliance with federal rules and regulations often constrains innovation. The reauthorized ESEA contains many new provisions designed to enable and encourage teachers to carry out instructional programs that best meet the needs of their students. For example, a comprehensive new waiver authority allows the Secretary of Education to waive ESEA provisions and regulations that impede reform, based on applications from states and school districts.

In addition, the department proposed — and the Congress agreed with some slight modification — to expand eligibility for Title I schoolwide program operation by lowering the eligibility threshold from 75% poverty to 50%. Schoolwide programs allow schools to use Title I funds to serve all children in a school; they also permit schools to combine ESEA and other federal resources to create comprehensive strategies for improving teaching and learning. In addition, the reauthorized bilingual education program offers new, comprehensive grants to schools and districts that enable them to provide bilingual education services to all students without regard to categorical distinctions.

Other adopted flexibility provisions include a new authority to support charter schools in states that have legislative authority to establish them, a provision allowing consolidated plans for all of the ESEA state programs, another provision to allow districts to use a small percentage of one program's funds for a second program, and provisions for state and local agencies to commingle administrative funds.

For Title I, this added flexibility will be accompanied by a more focused system of accountability. State assessments based on the state's standards and given at several key grade levels will replace the current system of yearly standardized test administration for all Title I students. This should help reduce the strain and loss of time from repeated testing while providing better information about students' progress toward meeting the standards. More important, it aligns the Title I accountability system with the state's assessment system. New assessment data then can be used by teachers, parents, schools, and school districts to make informed decisions about how to improve teaching and learning.

4. *Stimulate links among schools, parents, and communities.* One of the challenges in implementing any school reform is to involve parents, businesses, social service organizations, and other community stakeholders in a lasting, coordinated effort to help all children reach high standards. Both research and common sense show that children who read with their parents on a regular basis tend to perform well in school, and that children who are hungry, absent a great deal, or who feel unsafe at school tend to perform at lower levels.[19]

As proposed and passed, the IASA attempts to encourage parent and community involvement through several provisions. Title I parent-school compacts, developed by school staff and parents, will outline the common expectations and reciprocal responsibilities of parents and schools for helping students achieve. These compacts, to be discussed at parent-teacher conferences, are intended to help start an ongoing dialogue between parents and teachers about ways they can work together. Schools and parents also will develop a parent involvement plan to inform parents about school policies and practices and to offer training opportunities so that parents can learn strategies to help their children meet the standards.

Congress also ratified the Administration's proposal for a new Safe and Drug-Free Schools and Communities Act to support comprehensive, community-developed plans to prevent violence and drug abuse. Emphasis in the act is placed on involving social service agencies, community-based organizations, law enforcement, and others in the development and implementation of prevention strategies. Other provisions, including one allowing districts to use up to 5% of their funds to coordinate activities involving schools and local social services, were added by Congress.

5. *Target resources to where needs are greatest and in amounts sufficient to make a difference.* The challenge to target funds to high-poverty areas — and thus to reduce or eliminate Title I funding to school districts with little poverty — was the most politically contentious aspect of the Administration's proposal. Data since the early 1960s have shown that, other things being equal, low-income students in high-poverty schools suffer a dual disadvantage in achievement.[20]

Not only do these students suffer from a lack of resources in the home, but low expectations and few resources for professional development, instructional material, and basic supplies in these schools conspire to perpetuate low achievement.

The Administration proposed both to increase the amount allocated for the Title I program and to raise the amount that high-poverty districts receive by narrowing the number of school districts served by Title I. Title I funds would be further targeted to high-poverty schools through a "within-district" method of allocation, in which districts would rank all schools according to poverty level and then be required to serve all schools with poverty rates of at least 75%.

Targeting these funds would have resulted in some school districts and states losing a significant portion of the money they currently receive. While many members of Congress supported the concept of targeting, few were willing to sacrifice funds from their own districts. The final compromise formula between the House and Senate maintained current levels of funding for most districts, while including the possibility of some modest targeting of new appropriations to schools with higher levels of poverty. Within districts, the targeting accomplishments were mixed, though all schools with poverty levels of more than 75% must be served before schools with lower poverty rates are served.

The potential changes presented great challenges to Congress for the reauthorization of ESEA. Many educators and policy makers agreed that ESEA programs needed improvement; but the types of changes necessary, and their perceived risks, created considerable tensions throughout the reauthorization. For example, the emphasis on raising standards and expectations for Title I students while providing schools with increased flexibility in designing and administering Title I programs led some liberal members of Congress and civil rights advocacy groups to fear that services would be diluted and that certain populations would not be served. This led to the inclusion in the final legislation of many more specific requirements than proposed by the Administration. On the other hand, some conservative members of Congress were worried that an emphasis on state standards would inhibit local control over the school curriculum. The battle over "opportunity to learn standards" in Title I exemplified this concern. However, because evaluations and other research found that many of the previous ESEA programs were ineffective, there was a powerful case for making many of the changes proposed by the Administration.

The final stages of ESEA reauthorization lasted well into the fall of 1994. Because that was a heated campaign season for many members of Congress, the inevitable politicization of education issues and ESEA was even more pronounced. The raw politics of the Title I funding formula produced great tension among members, all of whom were eager to return home with funds for education. But perhaps the greatest sound and fury were over House and Senate floor amendments that had little to do with ESEA itself or with teaching and learning. Despite traditional conservative rhetoric about local flexibility and decision making, Senator Jesse Helms and Representatives Hancock and Johnson led fights to ban federal education funds from school districts that "taught or condoned homosexuality" or prohibited "Constitutionally protected prayer," regardless of the funds — local, state, or federal — used for such activities.[21] However, in the end, guided by the leadership of the authorizing committees and their staff, the Congress affirmed most of the components of the Administration's proposal.

In many ways the new ESEA can be thought of as providing federal assistance to give all students the opportunity to learn to challenging state standards. The new ESEA supports state and local reform, provides special help to the most needy students to achieve to high state and local standards, provides new resources and strategies to enable teachers to teach more challenging curricula, focuses attention and resources on making schools safe and drug free, and provides local schools with the flexibility to use imagination and creativity in teaching their students.

While substantially redesigning programs posed challenges on Capitol Hill, the real process of change — program implementation — is only now under way. At the federal level, the Department of Education is re-examining the regulations process, making a concerted effort to issue only those regulations required by law. Development of guidelines for consolidated applications, waiver approval, and other flexibility provisions have led the Education Department to think creatively about the various shapes reform may take and how best to support state and locally driven reforms while also promoting opportunities for all children — particularly those in need — with access to high-quality teaching and learning that will help enable them to reach challenging standards.

The reality that great disparities exist among schools further complicates reform efforts. Reducing the learning gap between high-poverty and low-poverty schools while also encouraging higher standards will require tremendous effort and commitment. Content and performance standards adopted by many states already have begun to demand more of students and teachers, yet standards also will not ensure excellence. Opportunities and resources for teacher professional development, access to high-quality learning materials, and other resources are critical to providing all students with a real opportunity to achieve. Some advocates fear that reform based on new high standards will lead to increased disparities in performance, which may be true in the early years before widespread, consistent improvements take hold. However, over the long run, unless standards are clear, challenging, and universal, we believe that the nation will continue to tolerate a watered-down curriculum for our least advantaged.

Perhaps the greatest frustration in implementing school reform is the time it will take. Teachers will need time to learn new content and pedagogy; students will need to adjust to new educational demands. Reform efforts will, like all new systems, need constant examination and refinement. Their ultimate success will depend on the willingness of all involved to persevere in what Milbrey McLaughlin and Richard Elmore have called the "steady work" of change and improvement. The National Council of Teachers of Mathematics, for example, spent nearly five years drafting the mathematics standards, and they are still working to disseminate and help train teachers in the use of those standards. Vermont has invested several years and a great deal of effort and resources to train teachers in the use of portfolio assessments that have yet to be perfected.

It is in this context of the need for sustained support that the current political situation, especially on Capitol Hill, becomes most alarming. In order to fulfill conflicting campaign promises to cut taxes, balance the budget, and reduce the deficit, many lawmakers have threatened major cutbacks in funding for education. Lack of information, misinformation, and calculated, politically-oriented maligning of the Department of Education may provide fodder for campaign debates. But political gains will come at great cost to the many children in need of better education, as well as to the future of our economy and our democracy. Goals 2000 and ESEA earned bipartisan support as they worked their way through Congress. Clearly, there exists some common ground on fundamental issues of school reform.

The 1994 reauthorization of ESEA embodied a significant shift in the federal role in education while simultaneously reaffirming the basic principles on which the first ESEA was founded. The new ESEA reshapes federal programs in support of state and local reforms, while it helps safeguard both equity and excellence for disadvantaged students by insisting that they learn to the same challenging state standards as all other students. Together, Goals 2000 and ESEA can support major improvement in American education. The next step is harnessing that potential to make high-quality teaching and learning a reality for all our children.

Footnotes

1. See P.L. 103-382.
2. See Carl Kaestle and Marshall S. Smith, "The Federal Role in Elementary and Secondary Education, 1940-1980," *Harvard Education Review* 52 (November 1982): 384-408.
3. Stephen K. Bailey and Edith K. Mosher, *ESEA: The Office of Education Administers the Law* (Syracuse, N.Y.: Syracuse University Press, 1968).
4. Ruby Martin and Phyllis McClure, *Title I of ESEA: Is It Helping Poor Children?* (Washington, D.C.: Washington Research Project, and New York: NAACP Legal Defense and Education Fund, 1969). One of the interesting historical sidebars is that one of the authors of this study, Phyllis McClure, also had a major influence on the ESEA reauthorization of 1994, as well as on the intervening reauthorizations.
5. Carl Kaestle and Marshall S. Smith, "The Federal Role in Elementary and Secondary Education, 1940-1980," *Harvard Education Review* 52 (November 1982): 384-408.
6. Michael S. Knapp, ed., *Better Schooling for the Children of Poverty, Alternatives to Conventional Wisdom: A Study of Academic Instruction for Disadvantaged Students, Volume I, Summary* (Menlo Park, Calif.: SRI International; Washington, D.C.: Policy Studies Associates, 1992). M.S. Knapp, P.M. Shields, and B.J. Turnbull, *Academic Challenge for the Children of Poverty* (Washington, D.C.: U.S. Department of Education Planning and Evaluation Service, 1992).
7. J.A. O'Day and M.S. Smith, "Systemic School Reform and Educational Opportunity," in *Designing Coherent Education Policy: Improving the System*, edited by Susan Fuhrman (San Francisco: Jossey-Bass, 1993). M.S. Smith and J.A. O'Day, "Educational Equality: 1966 and Now," in *Spheres of Justice in American Schools: The 1990 American Education Finance Association Yearbook*, edited by Deborah Vertegen and James Gordon Ward (New York: HarperCollins, 1991).
8. Brenda Turnbull, Shepard Zeldin, and Todd Cain, *State Administration of the Amended Chapter 1 Program* (Washington, D.C.: U.S. Department of Education, Office of Planning, Budget and Evaluation, 1990). Brenda Turnbull, Marjorie Wechsler, and Eric Rosenthal, *Chapter 1 Under the 1988 Amendments: Implementation from the State Vantage Point* (Washington, D.C.: U.S. Department of Education, Office of Policy and Planning, 1992). Wayne Riddle, *Education for Disadvantaged Children: Reauthorization Issues*, Congressional Research Service Report for Congress, Issue Brief 87070 (Washington, D.C.: U.S. Library of Congress, Congressional Research Service, 11 January 1989).
9. The National Council on Education Standards and Testing, *Raising Standards for American Education: A Report to Congress, the Secretary of Education, the National Education Goals Panel, and the American People* (Washington, D.C., 1992). One of us, Smith, was on the council and was the chair of the panel that prepared the recommendations on standards.

10. Jennifer A. O'Day and Marshall S. Smith, "Systemic School Reform and Educational Opportunity," in *Designing Coherent Education Policy: Improving the System*, edited by Susan Fuhrman (San Francisco: Jossey-Bass, 1993). U.S. Department of Education, *Reinventing Chapter 1: The Current Chapter 1 Program and New Directions, Final Report of the National Assessment of Chapter 1* (Washington, D.C., 1993).

11. Michael S. Knapp et al., *The Eisenhower Mathematics and Science Program: An Enabling Resource for Reform* (Washington, D.C.: U.S. Department of Education, 1991). Joan Ruskus et al., *How Chapter 2 Operates at the Federal, State, and Local Levels* (Washington, D.C.: U.S. Department of Education, 1994).

12. John F. Jennings, ed., *National Issues in Education: Goals 2000 and School-to-Work* (Bloomington, Ind.: Phi Delta Kappa and the Institute for Educational Leadership, 1995).

13. Michael G. Fullan, with S. Stiegelbauer, *The New Meaning of Educational Change* (New York: Teachers College Press, 1991). D. Osborne and T. Gaebler, *Reinventing Government: How the Entrepreneurial Spirit Is Transforming the Public Sector* (New York: Plune, 1993). Arthur A. Thompson and A.J. Strickland III, *Strategy Formulation and Implementation: Tasks of the General Manager* (Homewood, Ill.: Richard D. Irwin, 1992).

14. Linda Darling-Hammond, "Instructional Policy into Practice: The Power of the Bottom Over the Top," *Education Evaluation and Policy Analysis* 12 (Fall 1990): 233-42.

15. Presidential Transition Team, Education, Labor and Humanities Cluster, *Report of the K-12 Transition Team to the Incoming Assistant Secretary for Elementary and Secondary Education*, January 1993.

16. Commission on Chapter 1, *Making Schools Work for Children in Poverty: A New Framework Prepared by the Commission on Chapter 1* (Washington, D.C.: Council of Chief State School Officers and American Association for Higher Education, 1992). U.S. Department of Education, *Reinventing Chapter 1: The Current Chapter 1 Program and New Directions* (Washington, D.C.: U.S. Department of Education, Office of Policy and Planning, Planning and Evaluation Service, February 1993).

17. U.S. Department of Education, *Improving America's Schools Act of 1993: Reauthorization of the Elementary and Secondary Education Act*, Prospectus (Washington, D.C., 1993).

18. David K. Cohen, Milbrey W. McLaughlin, and Joan E. Talbert, eds. *Teaching for Understanding: Challenges for Policy and Practice* (San Francisco: Jossey-Bass, 1993). Andrew Hargraves and Michael G. Fullan, *Understanding Teacher Development* (New York: Teachers College Press, 1992). Judith W. Little, "Teacher Professional Development in a Climate of Educational Reform," *Educational Evaluation and Policy Analysis* 15 (1993): 129-51. Lee S. Shulman, "Teaching Alone, Learning Together: Needed Agendas for the New Reforms," in T.J. Sergiovanni and John H. Moore, eds. *Schooling for Tomorrow: Directing Reforms to Issues that Count* (Boston: Allyn and Bacon, 1989). Joan W. Talbert, *New Strategies for Developing Our Nation's Teaching Force and Ancillary Staff with a Special Emphasis on the Implications for Chapter 1* (Washington, D.C.: U.S. Department of Education National Assessment of Chapter 1, 1992).

19. U.S. Department of Education, *Teacher Survey on Safe, Disciplined, and Drug-Free Schools* (Washington, D.C., 1991).

20. Abt Associates, "Prospects: The Congressionally Mandated Study of Educational Growth and Opportunity," unpublished tabulations reported in *Reinventing Chapter 1: The Current Chapter 1 Program and New Directions* (Washington, D.C.: U.S. Department of Education, 1993).
21. Several versions of both the school prayer amendment and the sex education amendment were proposed and debated on the floor of both the Senate and the House before the conference. The final version of the school prayer section in the Improving America's Schools Act can be found in the General Provisions section (P.L. 103-382, Sec. 14510, 108 stat. 3906. 20 U.S.C. 8900); it is followed by the final version of the sex education section (P.L. 103-382, Sec. 14511, 108 stat. 3906, 20 U.S.C. 8901).

A Nickel on the Dollar

By Richard P. Mills

Richard P. Mills has served as the Vermont Commissioner of Education since March 1988. Prior to assuming that role, Mills served as education advisor to Governor Thomas H. Kean of New Jersey and directed the governor's national education work.

Mr. Mills serves on several boards, including the National Center on Education and the Economy, the New Standards Project, and the National Assessment Governing Board.

Mr. Mills earned master's degrees in history and business administration and an Ed.D. in educational administration from Columbia University. He was a history teacher and, in 1971, joined with four other teachers to found an independent school in New York City. He also has held adjunct teaching appointments at Columbia University and Rutger's University.

When Secretary of Education Richard Riley was governor of South Carolina, he started an annual publication called, *What the Penny Buys*. It was his effort to show the education results supported by an additional penny on the sales tax in his state. That example comes to mind as I think about the emerging federal role in education.

The federal government sends Vermont only five cents on the dollar for education. But it is a very important nickel, and it is more important now than ever before. The basis for that odd conclusion is the fact that something remarkable has been achieved in the last two years in education policy.

Tiny Vermont spends more than $700 million to educate its children. Only about $35 million comes from an array of federal sources. How can so little be so important? The explanation is not to be found in the numbers of school lunches served, children with Title I services, or children with special education. If we look only at those data, there often appear to be more problems than advances. What school leader is without a list of children not served, mandates unfunded, paperwork gone awry?

The extraordinary public policy achievement in education in the last two years has been the emergence of a consensus on a reform strategy and the infusion of that strategy into all levels of the education system. This consensus is fragile, not at all widely understood or shared, and still untested. The payoff, if there is to be one, lies far in the future. But at least the partners are pulling in the same direction.

The importance of the federal nickel jumps out of the documents on my desk as I prepare for yet another legislative session in Montpelier. Vermont's strategic plan for education is *The Green Mountain Challenge.* The strategies that appear there certainly are not identical to those in Goals 2000, but they are similar. They also bear a resemblance to the opening sections of the Improving America's Schools Act (IASA), the draft education reform bill now before the Vermont legislature, and the strategic plans in Colchester, Vermont, and dozens of other places. A similar strategy also appears in the New American Schools Development Corporation's challenge, in the work of the Business Roundtable, and in the Carnegie Corporation's remarkable series of studies on elementary education, middle grades, and the emerging work on early education. The reform agenda also appears in every gathering of the National Alliance for Restructuring Education.

This consensus is a problem for some critics of the current view of reform. But the consensus did not emerge because the federal government used its nickel to force every other level of education into compliance. Rather, it resulted from a long effort among people at all levels. The federal partner came late to the game to support ideas that already were coming to life in many states and communities.

What Reform Agenda?

Policy leaders find it hard to remember that frontline educators and the general public have a very different view on reform efforts. The most common question from the practitioner is likely to be, How does this all fit together? The public is likely to be unaware of the reform agenda and conducts its own assessment every night when the child says, "School is boring." So what reform are we talking about?

Systemic reform embodies a vision of high skills for all students and a set of goals to make that vision come to life. It includes some version of this list of strategies: standards for student performance, transformed classroom practice to enable all students to reach the standards, accountability for results, high-performance management at all levels of the system, continuous professional development, deliberate effort to engage public support and participation in the reform, and joint ventures between human services and schools to ensure that, in the words of the first national education goal, all children arrive at school ready to learn.

Marc Tucker has pointed out that this is not a list of unrelated good ideas, but a set of connected strategies. The standards are the heart of the matter. Changes in classroom practice are intended to bring actual performance closer to the standards. The assessments measure performance in relation to the standards. Professional development should enable teachers and other educators to learn a wide array of practices that give them a greater chance of raising the performance of all students to those standards. And the human services connection reflects the realization that schools alone cannot get students to high skills.

It is a truism that education has been a fragmented enterprise. In the past, legislatures often considered only general fund dollars on the grounds that the federal funds were not only beyond control or influence but unrelated to state purposes. Most federal programs still have unique plans, rules, and reporting requirements. So the fragmentation will be with us for quite a while under the best of conditions. But we also can see the opportunity to link efforts at local, state, and national levels to the common purpose of high skills for virtually all students. That *is* new — and powerful.

Five years ago, a chapter on the federal role in education would have to be about a world apart from the experience of most classroom teachers and most state policy leaders. It would have involved entitlements, maintenance of effort, and a list of titles and acronyms beyond the understanding of all but the specialists. The federal government had its priorities, and we in the states had ours. That is no longer the case. The rest of this chapter turns to some critical elements of the reform strategy and examines the nature of the new partnership.

Building a Reform Agenda

There are many well-developed versions of systemic reform. Some reflect legislative responses to court cases, as in Kentucky; some reflect combined state and local efforts, as in Vermont; and others are completely local in inception.[1] The federal legislation did not start this, but it does add weight where it is needed most to support ongoing local and state reforms. Goals 2000 is a good example.

Goals 2000 is voluntary; but those states and communities that do participate receive funds to support planning in the first year and then, in following years, resources to bring those plans to reality. Goals 2000 avoided the tendency to spell out exactly how the plans should look. The Secretary of Education signaled the new approach by declining to develop rules to go with the legislation. The law was to be sufficiently clear to guide action. And it is.

States with reforms in the works can have their existing plans accepted as the basis for Goals 2000 funding. They do not have to start over. States and communities that have not been able to develop their own strategies find a clear outline — not a prescription — on how to get started in Goals 2000.

In Vermont, hundreds of people participated in crafting the reform agenda. And every 18 months or so we take *The Green Mountain Challenge* apart, examine the pieces, and put it together again with renewed force. As the Vermont Goals 2000 panel assembles, its charge is to add value to *The Green Mountain Challenge*, to fill any gaps, and above all to ensure that the public takes part in the education of children.

When new funding opportunities arise, whether in the form of challenges from the private sector, such as the New American Schools Development Corporation or IBM's Reinventing Education Challenge, or in response to the School to Work legislation, Vermont uses the same agenda. This is not only allowed by the new federal approach but positively encouraged.

This approach is not without dangers. Legislators ask, for example, whose agenda for reform is this? Has too much direction come from a national perspective and too little from the communities they represent? For Vermont, the best response is to point to the 4,000 people in the state who helped write the student standards, the hundreds of Vermont teachers who helped design national assessment systems, and the many opportunities Vermont citizens took to shape the national agenda.

Another danger is that expectations for federal support from Goals 2000 can never be realized in the short run. Vermont received only $400,000 to start the planning for the first year, while 60% of the funding came from the state level in the planning year. That is very little new money when one contemplates the losses in Chapter 2 funds. In the following year, it is unlikely that Vermont's share will exceed $1 million; and there is the very real possibility that Goals 2000 could be changed by a Republican-controlled Congress.

The nub of the matter is this: All communities that undertake to change their schools for high performance need to do three things.

They need to 1) define expectations for all students, 2) measure results against the expectations and talk sensibly about them, and 3) build capacity in every part of the system to get better results. All the rest of the elements of the systemic reform agenda are merely expansions of these three tasks. It is as simple as that. And as complex.

Great Expectations

Goals 2000 incorporated the work on national standards begun under the Bush Administration and created a structure at the federal level, the National Education Standards and Improvement Council (NESIC), to certify these standards and, on a voluntary basis, also state standards. IASA takes a consistent position by requiring each state to demonstrate that it has "developed or adopted challenging content standards and challenging student performance standards," and these are to be the same standards for all children as developed in response to Goals 2000.

Anyone familiar with the national standards sees the problem: There is just too much there. No student could master all the details in all of those standards, and no school schedule could encompass all the opportunities to learn that material. The panels that developed the standards did their work well, for the most part; but there has not yet been any discipline imposed, no sense of proportion applied to sort out the essential from the trivial.

Several attempts have been made to develop criteria for certifying the national standards. One of the first was Promises to Keep, which the National Goals Panel commissioned under the direction of Shirley Malcom. The Malcom group asserted that proposed standards should be world class, important and focused, useful, reflective of a broad consensus, balanced among such requirements as depth and breadth, accurate and sound, clear and usable, assessable, adaptable, and developmentally useful.[2]

A promising approach is one taken by the New Standards Project, which is a consortium of 18 states and large school districts. New Standards originally began to create a nationwide assessment system, and the members believed that the national standards would be the basis for the assessments. It has not happened that way. The standards panels have not created standards that are sufficient for test development. Consequently, New Standards has turned to drafting content standards created in the states.

Vermont's content standards have many authors. In all, more than 4,000 citizens contributed to the *Vermont Common Core of Learning*, a short pamphlet on what students should know and be able to do. This pamphlet describes 20 "vital results" in four categories: communication, problem solving, personal development, and social responsibility. Those vital results are to be played out in three fields of knowledge: mathematics, science, and technology; arts and humanities; and social sciences.

The Vermont Common Core is the public's plain-language answer to the endlessly repeated request to "think of a young person who is important to you and describe what you think that person should know and be able to do to succeed in the 21st century." The Vermont education profession then used the Common Core to create a Common Core Framework, which is a more detailed statement of the content standards needed to accomplish the intent of the Common Core. Attention now has turned to the performance standards that will make that content measurable.

Throughout the work on the Common Core Framework, designers pored over draft copies of the national content standards. We wanted the Vermont framework to be uniquely ours and, above all, to be faithful to what the 4,000 citizens said. But we also wanted it to be a bridge to the national standards. Making the bridge work is difficult, because the national standards are firmly rooted in the disciplines, while Vermont's approach is just as firmly multidisciplinary.

The New Standards Project draws on this kind of work in the states. Initial versions of New Standards are much simpler than the offerings of the national panels. One particularly attractive feature of the mathematics standards is that they begin with material that the general public would find reassuring: "Understands how to add, subtract, multiply and divide integers, rational and real numbers in commonly occurring forms: decimals, fractions, ratios." Then it goes on to include more complex topics of measurement, dimension, patterns, statistics, and probability.[3] Whether it was intended or not, this structure reflects the findings of the Public Agenda Foundation in *First Things First*, that the public accepts the need for high standards, provided that the basics are ensured along the way.[4]

New Standards may well complete the work of NESIC before that body even is appointed. New Standards faces the challenge of meshing differences among the states but operates totally free of the political concerns that delayed the NESIC appointments up to the time of this writing.

New Standards also has richly infused its work with firsthand information about the national standards in European and Pacific Rim nations. However, New Standards Project researcher Kate Nolan found that there really is no single statement of international standards that one can call up — an awkward point given the determination expressed in the National Education Goals to exceed international standards in a number of areas.[5]

The Improving America's Schools Act requires states to adopt standards that "contain coherent and rigorous content, and encourage the teaching of advanced skills."[6] Furthermore, the act requires challenging performance standards that are aligned with the content standards and distinguish among three levels of performance. These specifications are likely to be the most profound contribution of the new national effort — and the most likely to go astray. It is hard to overstate the complexity of creating these standards. Putting them in place will be even more difficult.

Once we make expectations clear in a way that can drive teaching practice, everything else about schools may change: time spent in class; selection of teaching methods, texts, and tests; and graduation requirements. State and federal regulations would take a completely different turn if we reached agreement on what students should know and be able to do. But the changes necessary to get to that point are so great that no one should be optimistic of success.

Measuring Results

States that take part in Goals 2000 must specify how they will measure and report results. The Improving America's Schools Act requires that each state plan demonstrates that the state has standards in mathematics and reading or language arts for each local education agency and school. These assessments must be the same for all children and aligned to the content and performance standards. One of the welcome changes in the act is the strong encouragement to states that are developing alternatives to the standardized tests. But Congress also listened to scholars and student advocates who are concerned that invalid and unreliable state assessments might be used in a manner that discriminates unfairly among students. Thus states have only a limited time to demonstrate that their new performance assessments pass technical criteria.

In spite of this encouraging development, this is a perplexing time for the entire assessment community. Local school boards keenly feel their responsibility to ensure local accountability. While teachers may be unaware of the scholarly community's dissatisfaction with traditional multiple-choice tests, many of them also reject the findings of the standardized tests that are disconnected from their curriculum. New Standards has brought its first reference exam on line and soon will have other components. But the project also must consider new ways to fund the development and administration of their assessments, because costs will be significant. The National Assessment Governing Board has a $70 million vision for the National Assessment of Educational Progress (NAEP) but only $26 million to support it. Thus the board must make painful choices about what to test and how often. Every state and many local communities face the same choices.

In Vermont, the State Board of Education adopted a three-year schedule to expand the assessment beyond writing and mathematics in the fourth and eighth grades. The constraint is not only money. The board must decide how to feasibly combine various assessments — portfolios, standardized tests, writing samples, NAEP, locally developed assessments, and other components to get a clear picture of student performance. Creating new assessments takes time; and the timetable established by the Improving America's Schools Act, while generous, is nevertheless challenging.

No entity — state, school district, National Assessment Governing Board, or any other single participant in the assessment effort — can afford the full-scale development and implementation of a complete assessment system. One of the unrealized opportunities of the 1990s is to build a consensus about the kind of assessment we need and can afford, and then to share the development costs and risks. The Council of Chief State School Officers and the New Standards Project have made credible attempts to do this, but the task of replacing a century of experience with standardized tests is far beyond the capacity of either group acting alone.

Building State Capacity

Having the right agenda is hardly more than a start. We need to organize to do the work, which means building capacity for systemic reform at every level in the education system. Education reform as it is now conceived cannot be accomplished by state agencies that stress compliance and regulation. Nor is it sufficient to reconceive the state education department as the helper. Change on the scale now envisioned requires a wholly different role for state education departments. This role demands vision, the continuous building of productive relationships, and the luck to pick the right levers on which to lean. As

Marshall Smith and Jennifer O'Day pointed out in their influential paper, the work of states is to establish vision and goals, a curricular guidance system, assessment, and supportive finance and governance systems.[7] Only some of these topics now engage the state departments of education, and even those few occupy a surprisingly small part of the departments' time.

Goals 2000 was conceived in part to build this state capacity. The initial year of the act provided that 60% of the funds should remain with the state. The chief state school officer shared equally with the governor in selecting the goals panel, and the state agency retained oversight for the implementation of the Goals 2000 plan. In practice, there are severe limitations. In Vermont, for example, the new Goals 2000 funds were little more than what had been lost by Chapter 2 reductions. Nevertheless, the process of developing an application and the forthright manner in which the U.S. Department of Education implemented Goals 2000 encouraged a rethinking of state-level expenditures.

The new federal actions occurred at a time when the Vermont Department of Education was midway though a complete re-creation of itself. The new organization that emerged from nearly two years of discussions was smaller and flatter. Its mission was explicit: The Department of Education existed to transform schools for high performance. We replaced a traditional hierarchical structure with six teams and several cross-department groups. Management positions dropped from 22 to 12. Each team was led by a pair of managers who worked in concert: an external manager responsible for relations with external customers and the policy environment and an internal manager responsible for the effective use of resources. The two management groups worked together on strategic planning and the implementation of the new organization. Every member of the department completed four days of training in certain concepts of Total Quality Management. In particular, we sought to develop common approaches to solving problems and improving the quality of ongoing processes.

Three times in the last two years we conducted extensive internal surveys to check our performance against our mission and shared values. The first results were positive and probably reflected the fact that the checks were made on the last day of a four-day training experience that was unprecedented for department members. The second survey six months later captured the organization in the early stages of a radical transformation, and the performance dip was there for all to see. A year later, we had returned to earlier levels of performance in the eyes of internal customers, although significant organizational issues remained. After the second and third checks, the data were prominently displayed throughout the organization, and management conducted a systematic examination of the data to identify actions to boost performance.

In the midst of these developments, the governor proposed a merger of the Department of Education and the Department of Employment and Training. This new agency would be under a cabinet secretary. The governor's proposal reflected his strong interest in workplace issues and economic development, but it also was a manifestation of a perennial issue for Vermont governors: how to exert management control over a department that consumed a third of the state's budget. Federal education policy made a strong backdrop for this issue, as we will see in the effect of School-to-Work.

In early 1995, a Vermont legislative study concluded that the Department of Education was a productive (albeit stressed) organization. But the primary conclusion in the report was that the state board, the administration, and the legislature held somewhat conflicting views on the appropriate mission of the Department of Education. How this will be resolved remains to be seen. The force of the federal role would seem to support an education department built around a mission of education change at the local level. However, the federal message on workforce policy also is a significant force.

How should the states organize to do the work of education reform? A stronger state education agency alone is not enough, and a new reporting mechanism along traditional state agency lines also is not the best solution. There are just too many partners, too much information, and too fast a pace for this kind of structure. A more promising approach appears to involve building extensive relationships among many state agencies and strongly following through with their local and regional partners. Several federal actions encouraged this, such as the federal support for the concept of human resource investment councils.

Do We Really Mean All Children?

One of the profound changes in the new federal education policy structure is the clear intent to educate all children to the same high standards. To many educators and members of the public, this makes little intuitive sense. Yet the Public Agenda Foundation discovered that the public in general welcomes this idea of high skills for all, provided that educators take care of "first things first." That is, the public will accept the quest for high skills, but they want to see the basics covered along the way. And they will support reform, provided that schools are safe and orderly.

The aspect of education in which the "all children" mantra is tested most vigorously is special education. Federal law has long pushed for inclusion. Across the nation, perhaps 40% of children with special needs are in regular classrooms. In Vermont, that figure is 84%, which is the highest in the nation.

Special education exists in large part because the federal government stepped in a generation ago where states and local communities had failed to act. In the face of federal entitlement backed by civil rights legislation, a whole system of special education arose to serve more than 10% of America's students — and a much larger percentage in some communities. In many ways, special education has become a separate and unequal system wherein standards, curricula, results, and costs are strikingly different from the programs experienced by other students. Nevertheless, federal law strongly encourages states and communities to educate students with special needs in the regular classroom wherever feasible.

Vermont built on many years of support for an inclusive approach to education in 1990, when the legislature passed Act 230, which removed the financial incentive to place students in special education. In essence, the new law provided schools with sufficient funds for an expected proportion of their students to be in special education. Communities that managed programs in such a way that they had a lower proportion of students in those programs could retain the funds for other kinds of remedial education. Communities that placed a higher proportion of students in special education had to make up the funding difference on their own. The law strengthened the capacity of the regular program to educate children with much more complex needs by taking 1% off the top of special education funding to pay for professional development for regular classroom teachers. The law also created child-support teams in every school to ensure that students had every chance to succeed in the regular program.

The result has been a dramatic decline in special education enrollments in Vermont. While all other states have increased the proportion of students in special education, Vermont's special education enrollment has dropped more than 18% in four years. This new pattern followed several years of 6% annual increases.

The federal government continues to be criticized for creating a bureaucratic tangle that makes special educators the most paperbound of all educators. However, the regulatory environment can be simplified. Vermont turned to five schools with the challenge to invent ways to cut the paperwork. A year later, they had transformed — all within federal guidelines — the way students are placed in special education and the whole relationship between parents and schools.

Schools found that they did not need to have a child-study team and a separate Individual Education Plan Team meet three times to draft a plan for a student. A single team that met only once could do the job. And that plan did not need to be a dozen or more pages long and written in legal jargon. Three pages would do. The combined local and state design team decided to build the entire student plan around three questions: 1) What do we know about this child? 2) What are we going to do about that? 3) How will we know it worked? The first question immediately makes the parent the expert. Consequently, the previously adversarial relationship was transformed into a joint venture to find the best education for a child. What started as a paper chase became a much simpler and more human approach to educating a child. The state board heard the report from the five schools, then a month later changed their regulations to make the new approach possible for all schools.

The story does not end there. Only 10% of Vermont children are in special education, but special education funds from state sources provide extra support of one kind or another for more than 30% of all students. The system succeeded in helping students without labeling them. But we must think anew about how to finance this. If students cannot get the help they need in any other way, parents and educators will have no choice but to fall back on federal entitlements that will quickly re-establish separate programs for these children at higher cost and with lower expectations for the children. It is, as Dennis Kane of the Vermont Department of Education says, an endangered success.

Getting Ready for Work

An emerging theme in federal education policy is creating a smooth transition from school to work. The Carl Perkins legislation has done much to pave the way for long-attempted changes in technical education, but it also created some obstacles. Nowhere in education has the federal government been more prescriptive than in this technical education legislation. There are many set-asides, and much of the money is driven toward special populations.

But there are so many positives as well. Carl Perkins provided the development funds for cash-strapped states and carried the idea of Tech

Prep throughout the nation, building bridges between technical schools and higher education. Perkins helped strengthen the early high school education of students who previously might never have considered postsecondary education. That act helped change the image of technical education from a low-skills track to a program that is, in some places, more demanding than all but the most rigorous college preparatory programs.

However, when Congress provided for the National Skills Standards Board in 1994, a new opportunity appeared. Marc Tucker has envisioned the creation of a three-tiered system of standards with level one representing those standards that all should achieve in high school, level two representing perhaps 30 "chunks" or skill clusters, and level three for specific job skills.[8] Level one is the work of the National Educational Standards and Improvement Council (NESIC). Level two is the proper work of the National Skills Board. Level three is no task for government at all. But Tucker also warns of the fate of nations that build skills lists by codifying what the majority of businesses currently use. The challenge, he says, is to ensure that the skills are those of the high-performance workplace. It is good advice and a good warning. Alas, the Skills Board has yet to begin its difficult work as of this writing.

Left to their own devices, states do exactly what Marc Tucker warns the national government to avoid. Many states have long lists of skills clusters, and the authors tend to be the industry groups. There is ample rhetoric about preparing for the high-performance future, but a quick scan of the lists reveals a more pedestrian present.

Vital Partnerships with Human Services

To parents, teachers, or former teachers, the first national education goal is the most arresting: Every child will arrive at school ready to learn. Bringing that goal to life has given new energy to complex links between education and human services at every level. Several years ago as a new administration began in Vermont, the commissioner of education and the secretary of the agency of human services discovered that there were almost 20 separate points of contact between their two operations. They immediately resolved to work together to strengthen those connections.

The work was daunting for many reasons. The two sides of the partnership had different funding mechanisms, delivery methods, and jargon. The pays scales were different and so were the hours of work.

Educators and human services professionals had very different histories and professional preparation. They also had a rich folklore about the follies of their opposite numbers.

We began simply by exchanging lots of visits — education leaders to meet human services managers. Human services met school principals, and there were joint presentations to the state board and the governor. We built programs together to spark local invention of joint programs to enable more children to get to school ready to learn. A dozen regional meetings took place with educators and human services providers to jointly develop a mission statement. The education commissioner and human services secretary made presentations at "grand rounds" at the two largest hospitals. They testified together before legislative committees, collaborated to win large grants; and when the state budgeting process pitted one agency against another, they forced budget making onto new ground by sharing all the budget documents and by mentioning each other's budgets favorably in appropriations testimony. And we became a team that trained together endlessly.

The federal policy structure encouraged this, often in unintended ways. For example, children have an entitlement for special education services that they do not have for human services. The human services community knows this very well and uses the law to secure services for children and families for which they cannot otherwise pay. The practice leads to frustration among educators who see their costs rise in ways they cannot control. But educators and human services providers are pushed together in the process. Medicaid is another structure that brings the two partners together. Human services knows how to milk the complex Medicaid formula for program support. Special education funds pay for many services that are more legitimately Medicaid expenditures. The human services/education partnership yielded a growing stream of federal funds, but only after still more joint planning and exchange of the most arcane knowledge.

There are so many other points of contact: programs for infants and toddlers, early education and Head Start, and joint data collection on the condition of children and families. All of this combined effort suggests the potential for a different kind of governance structure at the state and local levels. The Center for the Study of Social Policy has built the case for boards of children and families in place of separate structures for education and the myriad of human services agencies.[9] Why not consider joint statements of mission and outcomes, jointly prepared budgets, and continuous training for the whole team of professionals? The encouragement in Goals 2000 for collaboration between the sectors fell on ready ground.

The Problem of Bringing Reform to Scale

There is no trick in finding schools and communities that put all the pieces together. What is difficult is to move beyond the handful of pilot projects to change on a broad scale. Goals 2000 intends just that, though that instrument acting alone will never be sufficient. But the Goals 2000 funds were never intended to act alone. The Vermont Goals 2000 application mentioned the National Alliance for Restructuring Education or the New American Schools Development Corporation or the Statewide Science Initiative of the National Science Foundation on virtually every page. We cannot afford to have a separate reform agenda for each funding source. Rather, all must knit together. Schools do this also.

In spite of all of the discussion about systemic reform and all of the encouragement in federal and state policy, collaborative reform is still foreign to the experience of frontline educators, and many of the pieces just do not fit. Policy makers may see the connections between national goals and standards, standards and instructional strategies, and so on. But many teachers see the national goals only as a poster on the wall. They may be aware of the standards proposed by the National Council of Teachers of Mathematics, but they may be using a 1983 mathematics text written before the standards. While their latest professional development seminar was about performance assessment in relation to standards, the school calendar still includes a week of standardized testing that the teacher does not support intellectually and the general public does not understand.

There are no shortcuts, only the long slog of showing how the pieces fit, listening to the frontline perspective, making adjustments, celebrating small victories, enduring bitter setbacks, and finding new ways to work with an expanding group of partners. Patience is in short supply in American public life, and the current education reform effort has long since defied the odds of life expectancy. Implementation skills are important now, and they are also in short supply. Michael Fullan tells a wonderful anecdote about the government minister who is leaving office after having led the enactment of major education reform legislation. As he departs, he tells his successor, "Well, the hard work is done. We have the policy passed. Now all you have to do is implement it."[10]

So, this is the easy part?

Footnotes

1. Susan Follett Lusi, "Systemic School Reform: The Challenges Faced by State Departments of Education," in *The Governance of Curriculum: 1994 ASCD Yearbook* (Alexandria, Va.: Association for Supervision and Curriculum Development, 1994).
2. Shirley M. Malcom et al., *Promises to Keep: Creating High Standards for American Students: Report to the National Education Goals Panel* (Washington, D.C.: National Education Goals Panel, November 1993).
3. "New Standards Project Performance Standards," Draft (Learning Research and Development Center, University of Pittsburgh, and National Center on Education and the Economy, 29 November 1994).
4. Jean Johnson and John Immerwahr, *First Things First: What Americans Expect from the Public Schools* (New York: The Public Agenda, 1994), p. 15.
5. Kate Nolan, "Mathematics in France, 1994," Typescript, New Standards Project International Benchmarking (Learning Research and Development Center, University of Pittsburgh, and National Center on Education and the Economy, 31 May 1994). See also by the same author, "Mathematics in the Netherlands, 1994," "Mathematics in Japan, 1994," and "Mathematics in Sweden, 1994." In her presentation based on this material at the New Standards Governing Board meeting on 13-14 June 1994, Ms. Nolan indicated the absence of a single international standard.
6. *Improving America's Schools Act Conference Report to Accompany H.R. 6* (Washington, D.C.: U.S. Government Printing Office, 28 September 1994), p. 7.
7. Marshall S. Smith and Jennifer O'Day, "Systemic School Reform," unpublished draft, Stanford University, 22 October 1990.
8. Marc Tucker, *On Occupational Clusters, Or Early Thoughts on Organizing the Work of the National Skills Standards Board* (Washington, D.C.: National Center on Education and the Economy, April 1994).
9. *Changing Governance to Achieve Better Results for Children and Families* (Washington, D.C.: Center for the Study of Social Policy, 1994), pp. 14-16.
10. Michael G. Fullan, with Suzanne Stiefelbauer, *The New Meaning of Educational Change* (New York: Teachers College Press, 1991), p. 65.

Reinventing Education in the Image of the Great Society

By Bruno V. Manno

Bruno V. Manno is a Senior Fellow in the Education Policy Studies Program at the Hudson Institute in Washington, D.C. He previously served as Assistant Secretary of Education for Policy and Planning during the Bush Administration.

Mr. Manno directed the work of the team that developed America 2000, President Bush's strategy to achieve the National Education Goals. Mr. Manno began work in the Education Department in 1986 as director of planning for the Office of Educational Research and Improvement (OERI) and later held senior policy and management positions before being nominated as Assistant Secretary in 1992.

Mr. Manno received his B.A. and M.A. from the University of Dayton and his Ph.D. from Boston College. He is the author of numerous articles and reports.

The Clinton Administration could hardly contain itself. U.S. Secretary of Education Richard Riley reflected on two years of work at what "President Clinton calls. . . reinventing American education."[1] He crowed, "We passed more good education legislation than in the past 30 years."[2]

A department press release described the Administration's work as a "quiet consensus without much fanfare." It continued, "Inside the beltway, many Washington insiders say they're amazed. Not since the mid-'60s, veteran Capitol Hill watchers say, has so much been done for education."[3]

President Clinton was quick to join in. Heaping high praise on the Congress, he crooned, "I think this Congress will go down in history as a great Congress for education."

The usually politically correct *Washington Post* agreed. It said, "Whatever its record in other fields, the Congress. . . was highly productive in the field of education. Six bills were passed." Because of this "real achievement," the *Post* knighted them "an education Congress."[4]

The first victory in the education joust was the Goals 2000: Educate America Act, which the Administration called the "foundation of the Clinton education agenda."[5] Five other pieces of legislation followed, the final triumph being the Improving America's Schools Act (IASA). This 1,000-page, five-year rechartering of the federal government's main financial investment in K-12 education — the Elementary and Secondary Education Act (ESEA) — allows the federal government to spend up to $65 billion over five years on nearly 50 education programs.

Not everyone sees these legislative victories in glowing terms. Before Goals 2000 became law, former Secretary of Education William J. Bennett called it a "terrible piece of legislation [that] puts the interests of the education establishment above the interests of children. [It] would hurt, not help, the education reform movement. . . [and] render the federal government and the education unions virtually unchallenged control over American education."[6]

After the legislation was signed into law, former Secretary of Education Lamar Alexander — who also vigorously opposed Goals 2000 — had advice for those who have to deal with it: "I would treat it about the same way you would treat a fox dressed as a duck at a duck family reunion."[7]

Bennett and Alexander led a last minute effort to kill IASA. They called it, "the kind of pernicious legislation which, if it is enacted, will make American education worse, not better. It will set back the renewal of American education [and] make it more difficult for reform-minded Americans to do what needs to be done."[8] In fact, both Goals 2000 and IASA further an education agenda that:

- imposes a top-down, "Washington knows best" approach to transforming America's schools, thereby expanding federal control of and diminishing what communities and states can do in those schools;
- extends the national policy role and influence of education experts from interest groups at the expense of such civilian consumers as parents and elected officials;
- shifts education reform from a focus on academic results to resources, from what our children should learn to what education bureaucrats spend.

Secretary Riley inadvertently implied that this agenda is a throwback to the mid-1960s policies of the Great Society. Washington arrives on the doorsteps of communities and states bearing gifts. As with any gift from Uncle Sam, the long-term result will be more red tape and directives that impose rules and regulations on communities and states, which presumably cannot be trusted to decide what is best for their schools.

Rhetoric to the contrary, most of the Clinton education agenda will, on balance, harm rather than help elementary and secondary education. It undermines a bipartisan proposal about how to reform our schools set out first by the nation's governors in the mid-1980s. Its fundamental principle was based on what then-Governor of Tennessee Lamar Alexander called "some old-fashion horse-trading. We'll regulate less, if schools and school districts will produce better results."[9] Key to achieving this was leadership by a state's governor and citizens in its local communities.

That approach gathered further momentum in 1989, when President Bush invited the governors to meet at an education summit in Charlottesville, Virginia. Together, they agreed to set six national education goals that they would work to achieve by the year 2000.

What followed in 1991 was America 2000. This national movement to reach the goals and transform America's schools was a community-by-community strategy to further a bipartisan agenda that:

- develops high academic standards for all students by defining what we expect them to know and do;
- tests for accountability and measures whether students are learning to those standards;
- cuts federal red tape and deregulates the process of schooling to allow for the innovations and resourcefulness of educators and communities;
- shifts control of schools from the producers — the education "experts" — to "civilians," the education consumers — elected officials such as state legislators and mayors, as well as parents and business leaders;
- gives families more choices of many different schools.

These features contrast sharply with the reinvented Great Society strategy of the Clinton Administration. What "new" Democrat Bill Clinton did in both Goals 2000 and IASA is what we would expect from "old" Democrats and the business-as-usual crowd, those who control the schools and like them pretty much the way they are. For them, a good education program takes the most amount of money for the least amount of change.

What follows examines the main elements of the Clinton education agenda. I begin by discussing the single model of reform it wants to impose on the country: so-called systemic reform. Next I analyze Goals 2000 and IASA and how they "transformed a nationwide reform movement into [another 1960s Great Society] federal program."[10] Finally, I suggest what Congress should do to again take up the bipartisan agenda set out by the governors, which involves sending education home, returning control to families, schools, communities, and states.

Systemic Change: The Clinton Reform Model

In the words of Secretary Riley, Goals 2000 was the beginning of "a new [federal] partnership in American education" with state and local school systems.[11] This partnership is based on a "systemic approach" to education reform. Its most prominent advocate is the present Under Secretary of Education, Marshall S. Smith.

In writings published prior to his current tenure in the U.S. Department of Education (during the Carter administration he was Chief of Staff to the first Secretary of Education, Shirley Hufstedler), Smith and his colleague Jennifer A. O'Day acknowledge that systemic reform provides "a more proactive role for the centralized elements of the system."[12] It also leads to greater uniformity — they call it co-ordination and alignment — in "all parts of a state instructional system — core content, materials, teacher training, continuing professional development, and assessment."[13]

Particularly important to this view of the nation's education agenda are equity and fairness in distributing resources and services among districts.[14] This leads advocates of the systemic approach to call for ways to judge whether there are adequate money, programs, and other human and fiscal resources to educate children in every school, district, state, and, ultimately, the nation. To ensure broad-based equity nationally, a new type of school resource standard must be created. And so we now have delivery standards — or what the Clinton Administration euphemistically calls opportunity-to-learn standards.[15]

How will these standards be used?

Clearly, they are a way of obtaining financial and human resources. But they also are "legal criteria for assessing whether students had been provided due process and equal protection."[16] They are, then, "leverage for courts and advocates [and can lead to] actions that could be taken by courts, legislatures, and advocates against a district or state."[17]

Naturally, some mechanism is needed to police the system and enforce the sanctions that are part of this approach — to perform the watchdog function. Smith and O'Day propose regular school reviews by teams from outside the district to evaluate the quality of practices and resources. They speculate that perhaps a system of national inspectors — a strategy used in centralized Ministries of Education — would help in "enforcing common standards. . . and [be] a professional force in the political arena."[18]

All of this places a high premium on the proactive role of Washington, while minimizing state and local control and resourcefulness. It assumes that Uncle Sam knows what is best for states and communities and will do all that can be done when it comes to regulations and enforcement to make sure that they "toe the line."

Goals 2000: Educate America Act

This systemic approach is enshrined as national education policy in Goals 2000. Many groups within the education establishment welcomed it with open arms — always a bad sign for those committed to challenging the status quo in education. Gordon M. Ambach, executive director of the Washington-based Council of Chief State School Officers, called it the "most significant federal legislation in 30 years."[19]

On the other hand, social critic Irving Kristol describes it as an "expensive disaster" in the making. It proves Kristol's "first law of education reform": "Any reform that is acceptable to the educational establishment, and that can gain a majority in a legislature, federal or state, is bound to be worse than nothing."[20]

To be fair, there are a few provisions in the law that warrant some praise. For example, it writes into law the six national education goals established in 1989 by President Bush and the nation's governors. It also writes into law the National Education Goals Panel, established by President Bush and the governors to monitor progress toward achieving the goals.

But even with these, it chose not to leave well enough alone. For example, it adds two national goals whose rhetoric diverts attention from a focus on student achievement and measurable outcomes. It curtails the authority of the goals panel and, while giving it power to review decisions made by a new federal entity called the National Education Standards and Improvement Council (NESIC), requires a two-thirds majority to overturn NESIC decisions. It also expands the number of academic subjects suggested for mastery prior to high school graduation beyond the five named in the original goals, namely, mathematics, science, English, history, and geography.

Most of what it does will do little to reverse the essence of the nation's education problem today: Our young people are not learning nearly enough for their own or the nation's good.[21]

There are three particularly onerous provisions in the law.[22] First, new federal dollars available for Goals 2000 may not be used for at least the next three years for "high stakes" tests — those that have consequences. This means that states cannot use Goals 2000 money to develop tests that will be used for promotion, high school graduation, or admission to college. The result is neither a meaningful accountability system nor a national testing system. This is folly to those hoping to improve student achievement. It fails to provide students with any incentives to work hard. It creates a no-fault system with no consequences for failure or rewards for success.

Even American Federation of Teachers President Albert Shanker points out the problems with this approach. He says: "All of the standards, all of the other measures called for in Goals 2000 — curriculum development, assessment, professional development, parental involvement — will not mean a thing unless we attach stakes to students' achievement of standards. . . . When you have a system that basically says, 'It doesn't count'. . . you have a system that will not work. Right now, what students want — college admissions, jobs, and job training — is disconnected from their school work. And as long as it stays disconnected, our educational system will not work."[23]

Second, in judging educational quality, Goals 2000 puts more emphasis on "inputs," such as school spending, how teachers teach, and class size, than it does on outputs — the academic results students achieve. It does this by creating a process for developing national delivery or opportunity-to-learn standards that measure school resources. Rather than providing students with an opportunity to learn, they will provide states and communities with an opportunity to litigate. They will become the impetus for new lawsuits that drag states and communities into court to redistribute resources. They will become another form of a legal entitlement in education.

Litigation is not some far-fetched imagining. Consider the Alabama case where the state court ruled that the K-12 system is unconstitutional because it does not provide students with an adequate education. Judge Eugene Reese, in a 125-page opinion, lists criteria that the schools must meet, including "providing students with an opportunity to attain" sufficient skills to compete with students throughout the world and "sufficient understanding of the arts to enable each student to appreciate his or her cultural heritage and the cultural heritage of others."

Representative Bill Goodling (R-Pa.) said at a committee hearing on Goals 2000: "I agree with the concept that you need to have equal opportunity, but all I can see is the trips to the court."[24] On the other hand, Helen Hershkoff, an American Civil Liberties Union lawyer representing the plaintiffs, calls the decision, "a landmark because it recognizes that children have a right not only to an equitable education but also to an adequate education."[25] This language reflects a delivery standards approach.

Another clue to what can be expected comes from the U.S. Department of Education Office of Civil Rights (OCR) "compliance review" of the state of Ohio. OCR investigated whether Ohio's high school exit exam violated the civil rights of minority students who failed it in "disproportionate" numbers. Kenneth A. Mines, director of OCR's Chicago office, said: "[We need]. . . to determine whether minority students will be denied high school diplomas on the basis of race or national origin because they have not had fair opportunities to learn."[26] Ohio's were not rigorous exams pegged to Advanced Placement standards. Rather, they asked high school seniors to pass a proficiency test geared to the end of the eighth grade. Furthermore, the Ohio Department of Education reported that students who failed these tests missed, on average, 32 days of school during their junior year, with one-quarter of them missing 45 days (nine weeks) of school. Some students were given nine opportunities to pass the exam. And certain districts, like Cleveland, conducted remedial summer sessions, offering to pay those who attended. (Only about 10% of those in Cleveland who failed the exam bothered to attend.) At the time of the review, Ted Sanders, Ohio Superintendent of Public Instruction, commented, "Every state that is even thinking about setting standards has to be watching this and wondering how high we can set expectations."[27]

After much wrangling, OCR concluded that the exit exam was not racially discriminatory. Their agreement with Ohio requires the state to do nothing that it was not already doing. Mines insists that OCR will continue to explore equity issues related to standards and testing. In particular, unequal results on these high-stakes exams will be viewed as potential civil rights violations. The real message — the strong signal — is unmistakable. It is best summarized by Phyllis McClure, former director of Educational Programs for the NAACP Legal Defense Fund. Commenting on the OCR review, she said, "It's a warning signal for all the states. They're all going to have to face this."[28]

The third disturbing Goals 2000 provision involves creating a new federal bureaucracy composed almost exclusively of education experts who will perform several tasks, including the certification of state standards. As the earlier discussion of systemic reform suggests, developing education standards that states must eventually make part of their state plan for submission to the U.S. Department of Education requires a national mechanism to direct development and police enforcement. Naturally, its members need to be experts skilled at judging these arcane matters. Hence, the law establishes a 19-member panel — the National Education Standards and Improvement Council (NESIC) — to oversee the certification of education standards — including delivery standards — that states "voluntarily" submit. In reality, NESIC is a sort of national school board whose members are the usual education establishment suspects. There are no NESIC membership requirements for bipartisanship or lay control of education.

Harold Howe, a former U.S. Commissioner of Education and now senior lecturer emeritus at the Harvard Graduate School of Education, calls Goals 2000 an "elaborate bureaucratic structure that brings Uncle Sam into. . . the classrooms of 2½ million American public school teachers."[29]

In blocking the development of a "high stakes" exam system, emphasizing resource standards for schools at the expense of academic standards for students, and expanding federal control of education by the usual education establishment bureaucrats, there is not much "new" about the "new" Democrat Bill Clinton or his friends, the education Congress. He and his friends are "old" Democrats who merely are reinventing education in the image of the Great Society.

Improving America's Schools Act

IASA culminates the efforts of the Clinton Administration to reinvent education in the Great Society image of programs, spending, regulations, and subservience to Uncle Sam. This approach manifests itself in four primary ways.

First, IASA has a top-down, centralized view of the federal role, with Uncle Sam as central planner. The bill mandates that statewide education reform plans be submitted to the U.S. Secretary of Education for approval. Though ambiguously phrased, there is little doubt they are to describe a states' content standards (what students must know and do), performance standards (what student achievement is good enough to denote content mastery), and delivery or opportunity-to-learn standards (what resources — fiscal and human — communities will devote to ensuring that students achieve these standards). They also must include assessment plans tied to the standards and schedules, projecting what yearly progress will occur.

Local districts must develop their own reform plans for state approval. They are to be integrated into the plan sent to Washington. A myriad of details must be specified, including how districts coordinate health and social service programs, homeless children programs, preschool programs, and a host of other programs. They even must describe a parent involvement policy that includes topics to be discussed at parent-teacher conferences.

No matter that the Clinton Administration's rhetoric is about plans created locally from the "bottom up." It is Uncle Sam who sets the requirements, describes the contents, writes the rules, and controls the purse strings. It is "top down" plain and simple, much like the centralized education ministries of many European and Asian countries.

Imposing the Administration's "systemic model" of school reform on the country makes Uncle Sam the country's central education planner. It is ironic to have the Clinton Administration advocate centralization when public and private organizations and institutions throughout the world see central management and top-down planning as failed endeavors. Taking their place are market-driven approaches that decentralize, eliminate bureaucratic administrative layers, and encourage local control and decision making.

Second, IASA further expands the federal power grab begun in Goals 2000 by dictating and micromanaging what communities and states are required to do. In Goals 2000 this power grab was evident especially in the creation of NESIC, with its authority to certify what content, performance, and delivery standards receive the federal seal of approval. This federal power grab is the height of arrogance. It makes schools accountable to Uncle Sam, bypassing the day-to-day wishes and inclinations of local communities. As night follows day, this meddling and intrusiveness will lead to new federal mandates, controls, and regulatory burdens on states and communities.

The Administration claims this interpretation is unjustified. Secretary Riley comments, "I strongly disagree with [the] belief that [our education package] will federalize American education."[30] But consider this example from ESEA. Any district receiving funds must expel from school for at least one year students found to have brought a weapon to school. Does an incident like this require a swift and sure response? Most certainly so. But should it be the job of Uncle Sam in

Washington to mandate a national policy on weapons and school expulsions for every school district and to impose it on all states and communities? Are local school boards, communities, and families too stupid to devise their own solutions to this problem? Most certainly not.

Even the mainline education establishment groups believe this intrusiveness is troubling. Bruce Hunter, senior associate executive director of the American Association of School Administrators, says: "The trend is worrisome, and they don't seem able to control themselves. This Congress has been more willing than ever to be the county council, the mayor's office, or the school board."[31]

Third, IASA reinforces another onerous aspect of Goals 2000 and the systemic model that favors control of education by bureaucrats and interest groups. Goals 2000 placed NESIC under the control of the education establishment. ESEA continues this move to expand the national policy role, influence, and control of bureaucrats and interest groups. For example, the National Assessment Governing Board now will have its members chosen by education interest groups. Placing the only testing program in the U.S. with a long record of objectively monitoring student learning under the control of bureaucrats and interest groups is like putting the fox in the same pen as the ducks. Today, the education foxes are smiling broadly.

Another example of interest group control is ESEA's Gender Equity Act, which mandates teacher training in "gender sensitivity [and] gender equitable practices." This politically correct provision panders to the wishes of a major interest group and is based on spurious research.[32]

In short, ESEA — like Goals 2000 — places control of education in the hands of education's producers rather than parents and other consumers, experts rather than lay people, bureaucrats rather than "civilians." "Systemic reform" is nothing more than many of the same old bureaucrats talking to many of the same old interest groups. In all likelihood, they will produce the same old results.

Fourth, IASA carries even further the Goals 2000 and systemic approach to judging quality in education by focusing on intentions and efforts, institutions and services, resources and spending, rather than goals and ends, products and results, and what students learn. It does this by proposing to put education spending on autopilot and send it into the stratosphere.

IASA would increase the total share of federal spending on education at least 1% each year until it reaches 10% of the federal budget. This year alone, the 10% formula would add about $130 billion to the federal education budget. No improvement in student learning would need to occur for this to happen.

There are numerous other windfalls for the education establishment. Targeted are the "professional development" types, especially the colleges of education. They would reap professional development money from at least two new sources: the reconfigured Eisenhower Professional Development Program and a mandated 10% "set aside" for professional development of teachers in low-income schools that have not made adequate progress in reaching agreed-on student achievement goals.

Sending Washington Home

ESEA, like much of this Administration's education agenda, is business as usual. Reinventing education in the image of the Great Society has one main effect. It undermines the bipartisan proposal about how to reform our schools first put forward in the mid-1980s by the nation's governors, furthered later that decade by the establishment of six national education goals, and advanced in the early 1990s by America 2000's community-by-community strategy to reach the six national goals.

There are those who try to gloss over or deny any difference between the Administration's perspective and this bipartisan approach. For example, one proponent of this view, John F. Jennings, says, "Goals 2000 is the child of Mr. Bush's America 2000 plan."[33] Nothing is further from the truth.

America 2000 was about voluntary national goals and high academic standards in core subjects for all students; gubernatorial leadership linked with local responsibility, freedom, and accountability in reaching the goals; tests that tell us whether students are learning to the standards and that have consequences for promotion, graduation, and employment; and wide ranging choices for families among public and private schools that differ on many dimensions.

Goals 2000 (and by implication, its companion piece, IASA) proposes national delivery standards that focus on money, not results, and on standards for schools, not standards for students; forbids the use of federal money to develop "high stakes" exams; expands Washington's role in education by creating a new federal bureaucracy that is akin to a national school board; and allows public school choice only when both the sending and receiving schools consent to the family request.

According to former Secretaries of Education Bennett and Alexander and Senator Dan Coats, "By signing off of H.R. 6 and Goals

2000, President Clinton transformed a nationwide reform movement into a federal program."[34] In other words, it made a true partnership with the states and the nation's governors into another bureaucratic and regulated intrusion from Washington.

Much of what the Clinton Administration has done in education involves a federal power grab for Washington and its allies in the education establishment. It substitutes the judgments of Uncle Sam and the Washington-knows-best crowd — especially the education experts — for those of lay people and civilians — especially families — in states and communities. Decisions made in Washington are substituted for those made by families, schools, communities, and states.

Ironically, this comes at a time when the public's trust of government in Washington is at an all-time low. The report of a 1994 survey conducted for the Hudson Institute's Project on the New Promise of American Life summarizes a 36-year trend:

> Today, when Americans are asked how much of the time they trust government to do what is right, only 2 percent say 'all the time' and just 14 percent. . . 'most of the time.' This reflects the lowest level of trust ever measured for government in Washington. . . more than one of five. . . trust Washington 'almost none of the time,' an equally damning finding.[35]

Another dimension of the "trust in government" issue is seen in a question that asks which branch or level of government has or should have the most power today. About 55% said that Congress has the most power, and state and local governments are named by fewer than 10%. However, 41% believed that state and local governments should have the most power; only 29% believed that Congress should have the most power.[36] This was true across the demographic and ideological spectrum.

One conclusion is clear. Transferring or devolving power back to states and communities — in other words, sending Washington home — receives significant backing from many Americans.

And what changes do Americans think should be made in their schools? In recent years a fairly consistent perspective has been present.[37] According to the most recent data:

- 89% say that developing the best education system in the world is essential to America's future strength, more important than the most efficient industrial system (60%) or the strongest military (40%);

- 81% favor requiring public schools in their community to conform to national achievement standards and goals;
- 70% favor the use of standardized national tests to determine if a student may advance to the next grade level — with 72% wanting to rank the local public schools by student achievement;
- 77% think federal agencies should give local authorities more say in how the money they receive is spent; and
- 62% favor allowing families to choose which public schools students attend in their communities, with even stronger support for this policy among minorities (70% for blacks, 66% for Hispanics) and inner-city residents (70%).

A report by Public Agenda adds another dimension to this discussion.[38] It shows that school "experts" do not share the public's top education concerns. While there are some extreme views on both sides of almost every education issue, the general adult population and white, African-American, and traditional Christians who are public school parents all have mostly the same education interests. They want safe schools where discipline is enforced and students master the basics before moving on to other things. Because of this, large majorities of Americans "are uncomfortable with many of the changes" being wrought on their children by education "experts." This includes changes like teaching composition without teaching spelling or the exclusive use of calculators to teach math, rather than insisting on both rote learning and calculators. This "traditionalism," though, does not lead them to yearn for "the good old days."

The report reaches conclusions similar to the American Dream findings on the issue of trust in government, but this time applied to education. Fifty-eight percent of Americans do not trust elected officials in Washington to make decisions about how schools should be run. (An interesting related finding is that 41% do not trust their state's governor to do this.) With all this in mind, what should the federal reform agenda be in K-12 education?

In brief, it should pursue a two-part agenda involving the politics of liberty and sociology of virtue.[39] The politics of liberty would roll back the huge expansion of federal involvement, bullying, and regulating in education that began with the Great Society. This includes implementing any needed structural, legislative, and constitutional changes. Relimiting the federal role in education goes beyond getting government off people's backs. It returns power and decision making to state and local governments and those institutions in civil society that nurture the character of its citizens.

Curbing government has its complement in the sociology of virtue — undertaking actions to strengthen and reinvigorate our civic and social institutions. These institutions are "mediating" structures, such as family, church, neighborhood, and the many voluntary associations that are so much a part of life in America. They often are more able than government to find solutions to what ails us, because they are closer to the problems and the people involved.

Undergirding both elements of this agenda is the principle of subsidiarity. It affirms that problems should be solved "as close to home" as possible.

Practically, what does this mean for Congress as it looks at K-12 education? Chester E. Finn Jr. suggests that a federal education package passed by the Congress that tries to send education home will have three parts.[40]

First, restore local control and undo the worst damage. Turn back both the Goals 2000 and IASA federal power grab by repealing much of the damage they do. To start, abolish the National Education Standards and Improvement Council (NESIC) and restore the bipartisan nature and independent authority of the National Education Goals Panel (NEGP), the governor's group that tracks the nation's progress toward achieving the national goals. Restore, too, the independence of the National Assessment Governing Board (NAGB), the policymaking group for the nation's report card on student achievement. All this would do much to squelch the return of the "experts" to a primary role in controlling national education policy.

Return the national education goals to the original six. The additions dilute the focus on improving student achievement by raising resources and measuring results. Bar Uncle Sam from doing most everything that interferes with local control of standards, curriculum, testing, and teaching. There are several examples of what Congress can do. To start, eliminate the requirement for establishing state improvement panels that create reform plans that Uncle Sam must approve. Eliminate, too, all references to opportunity-to-learn standards. And abolish the provision that restricts the use of federal money for developing "high stakes" tests.

Congress also should make it clear that civil rights enforcement involves protecting the rights of individuals and pursuing a color-blind society. It should not be based on solutions driven by spurious research on gender equity, race norming (the need to adjust test scores to compensate for characteristics like race or poverty), or other forms of politically correct group consciousness.

Second, send programs home. Most of the separate K-12 programs that now exist in the Department of Education and total approximately $10 billion should be sent home to states and communities. So should those that target such areas as special education. And so, too, should those that involve programs for children administered by other agencies, such as Head Start in the Department of Health and Human Services. The national research and development centers and the regional education laboratories — and myriad other forms of education "pork" for the experts — should be part of any package that goes to the states. They can use the money to purchase the research and school improvement services that they need.

Along with these programs, send home the means of paying for them. One option is to create a major "block grant" with few, if any, strings attached. Or swap programs with the states. They would receive a package of education programs while Uncle Sam takes full control of and responsibility for other areas, such as Medicaid. A third option is to reduce federal taxes with the expectation that states could substitute their own if they thought the programs worthy of support.

Decisions about what to do with these programs should involve broad consultation with the nation's governors. The final package could allow individual states some discretion in choosing which K-12 programs they may want returned to them, since no single approach is likely to meet every state's needs.

Third, eliminate the cabinet-level Department of Education. With many education programs returned to the states, there would be no need for a cabinet-level agency. What programs remain could be housed in an independent agency with a cabinet-level advisor in the White House reporting to the President.

Another option is to create something like an Office of Children and Families that includes other children's programs, such as Head Start. Some thought even could be given to re-creating a streamlined Department of Health, Education, and Welfare. Uncle Sam would continue to support some research and to collect statistics, especially relating to state, national, and international comparisons of education achievement. All this would support the gathering of necessary information to report on the nation's progress in achieving the national goals. There also would be a strong "bully pulpit" role, especially to single out what seems to be working or not working in efforts to transform our schools. Finally, the federal civil rights role should focus on pursuing antidiscriminatory actions involving individuals, not civil rights activism for various approved groups; this function could be transferred to the Department of Justice.

The point of all this is not to reduce the attention given to education by the nation. Rather, it is to focus that attention on encouraging and challenging families, schools, communities, and states to transform their schools because they — not Uncle Sam in Washington — are the only ones who can do that. The guiding principles for Washington in whatever functions it performs should be taken from the agenda of the American people: "choice, deregulation, innovation, accountability, and serious assessment keyed to real standards in core subjects."[41]

The Clinton Administration has reinvented education in the image of the Great Society and developed a Washington-knows-best agenda for transforming our schools. That approach may please education bureaucrats and experts. But it is sorely out of touch with what most Americans want for their schools.

The time has come — and the country seems willing — to have Washington send education home to where it belongs — families, schools, communities, and states. Rather than be incrementalist in its approach, the Congress (and perhaps even the Clinton Administration) now has an opportunity to be bold. The country will be better off for it.

Footnotes

1. Richard W. Riley, "A New Direction for Education," *Principal* (September 1993): 1.
2. "A Quiet Consensus to Improve American Education," *U.S. Department of Education News*, 1 September 1994, p. 1.
3. Ibid.
4. "An Education Congress," *Washington Post*, 18 October 1994, p. A16.
5. "The Clinton Education Agenda," *U.S. Department of Education News*, 13 October 1994, p. 2.
6. *Empower America*, press release, Washington, D.C., 23 February 1994.
7. *Education Week*, 30 March 1994, p. 16.
8. Memorandum to U.S. Senators on H.R. 6 from Lamar Alexander and William J. Bennett, *Empower America*, Washington, D.C., 5 October 1994.
9. National Governors' Association, *Time for Results: The Governors' 1991 Report on Education*, Washington, D.C., 1986, p. 3.
10. Lamar Alexander, William Bennett, and Dan Coats, "Local Options," *National Review*, 19 December 1994, p. 42.
11. Richard W. Riley, "Statement by Secretary of Education Richard W. Riley on GOALS 2000," U.S. Department of Education, 21 April 1993, p. 1.
12. Marshall S. Smith and Jennifer A. O'Day, "Systemic School Reform," in *The Politics of Curriculum and Testing: The 1990 Yearbook of the Politics of Education Association*, edited by Susan Fuhrman and Betty Malen (Bristol, Pa.: Falmer Press, 1991), p. 235.
13. Jennifer A. O'Day and Marshall S. Smith, "Systemic Reform and Educational Opportunity," in *Designing Coherent Education Policy*, edited by Susan Fuhrman (San Francisco: Jossey-Bass, 1993), p. 267.

14. Marshall S. Smith and Jennifer A. O'Day, "Systemic School Reform," pp. 245-46. See also Marshall S. Smith and Jennifer A. O'Day, "Educational Equality: 1966 and Now," in *Spheres of Justice in Education*, edited by Deborah A. Verstegen et al. (New York: Harper Business, 1991), pp. 53-100.
15. On the opportunity-to-learn issue, see Susan L. Traiman, *The Debate on Opportunity-to-Learn Standards* (Washington, D.C.: National Governors' Association, 1993); and Andrew C. Porter, "School Delivery Standards," *Educational Researcher* (June-July 1993): 24-30.
16. Smith and O'Day, "Systemic Reform and Educational Opportunity," p. 287.
17. Ibid., p. 285.
18. Ibid.
19. Rochelle L. Stanfield, "This Time, the Reforms Are for Real," *National Journal*, 30 April 1994, p. 1041.
20. Irving Kristol, "The Inevitable Outcome of 'Outcomes'," *Wall Street Journal*, 18 April 1994, p. A14.
21. For a sampling of evidence as well as other sources that support the view that this is the fundamental problem the schools face, see Scott W. Hamilton and Bruno V. Manno, "The Unfinished Work of School Reform," *Commonsense* (Summer 1994): 132-33. For a similar view published much earlier, see Albert Shanker, "A Proposal for Using Incentives to Restructure Our Public Schools," *Phi Delta Kappan* (January 1990): 346-47. For another similar but more recent view, see Chester E. Finn Jr., "What to Do About Education: The Schools," *Commentary* (October 1994), especially pp. 30-31.
22. For more detailed criticisms of Goals 2000, see: Michael Heise, "Goals 2000: The Federalization and Legalization of Educational Policy," *Fordham Law Review* 63 (November 1994): 345-38; Bruno V. Manno, "Goals 2000: Washington Knows Best," *Network News and Views* (May 1994): 57-58; Theodor Rebarber, "Goals 2000: Help or Hindrance?" *Network News and Views* (May 1994): 62-64.
23. Albert Shanker, *Making Standards Count: The Case for Student Incentives* (Washington, D.C.: American Federation of Teachers, 1994), pp. 5, 10.
24. Julie A. Miller, " 'Goals 2000' Gets Mixed Reaction," *Education Week*, 12 May 1993, p. 18.
25. Edward Felsenthal, "School System in Alabama Gets 'F' from Court," *Wall Street Journal*, 6 April 1993, p. B1; Peter Appleborne, "Its Schools Ruled Inadequate, Alabama Looks for Answers," *New York Times*, 9 June 1993, pp. A1, B7.
26. On the Ohio case, see the following: Lonnie Harp, "Curriculum Is Focus in Probe of Ohio Exam," *Education Week*, 6 April 1994, pp. 1, 10; Drew Lindsay, "No Racial Bias Found in Ohio's School Exit Exam," *Education Week*, 12 October 1994, pp. 1, 16; Carol Innerst, "Ohio Claims Quiet Win Over Education Department," *Washington Times*, 24 September 1994, p. A3; Albert Shanker, "Standards in Ohio," *New Republic*, 23 May 1994, p. 19.
27. Harp, op. cit., p. 1.
28. Lindsay, op. cit., p. 16.
29. Harold Howe II, "Uncle Sam Is in the Classroom," *Phi Delta Kappan* (January 1995): 374, 376.
30. Richard W. Riley, "Statement by Secretary Richard W. Riley on Education Issues Before the American Public, 1994," U.S. Department of Education, 13 October 1994, p. 5.

31. Mark Pitsch, "In Political Season, 'Social Issue' Add-Ons Bulk Up E.S.E.A.," *Education Week,* 26 October 1994, p. 22.
32. Lynn Olson, "Idea of 'Gender Gap' in Schools Under Attack," *Education Week,* 28 September 1993, p. 16; Christina Hoff Sommers, "Capitol Hill's Girl Trouble," *Washington Post,* 17 July 1994, pp. C1, C4; Christina Hoff Sommers, "The Myth of Schoolgirls' Low Self Esteem," *Wall Street Journal,* 3 October 1994, p. A18.
33. John F. Jennings, "What to Expect from a New Year and a New Congress," *Education Week,* 11 January 1995, p. 56. For a keen and comprehensive analysis of the differences between America 2000 and Goals 2000, see Diane Ravitch, *National Standards in American Education* (Washington, D.C.: Brookings Institution, 1995), pp. 135-86. See also Chester E. Finn Jr., "The Real Clinton Education Policy," *Education Week,* 25 January 1995, pp. 48, 38.
34. Alexander, Bennett, and Coats, op. cit., p. 42.
35. Frank I. Luntz, *The American Dream: Renewing the Promise* (Indianapolis: Hudson Institute, 1994), p. 7.
36. Ibid., pp. 9-10.
37. See especially Stanley M. Elam, Lowell C. Rose, and Alec M. Gallup, "The 26th Annual Phi Delta Kappa/Gallup Poll of the Public's Attitudes Toward the Public Schools," *Phi Delta Kappan* (September 1994): 42-56.
38. Jean Johnson and John Immerwahr, *First Things First* (New York: Public Agenda Foundation, 1994).
39. Though these two tasks are proposed in another context, they are equally valid in education. See William Kristol, "The Future of Conservatism," *The American Enterprise* (July/August 1994): 32-37. Kristol acknowledges his indebtedness to the sociologist Robert Nisbet for this formulation.
40. Chester E. Finn Jr., "A Primer for Education Reform," *Wall Street Journal,* 13 January 1995, p. A12. See also Lamar Alexander and William J. Bennett, "Abolishing the Department of Education in Order to Liberate Parents and Schools," Statement Before the House Economic and Educational Opportunities Committee, 26 January 1995. For a more general discussion of the federal role, see Chester E. Finn Jr., "A Tempest in a Teapot," *Harvard Graduate School Alumni Bulletin* (Summer 1968).
41. Alexander, Bennett, and Coats, op. cit., p. 44.

PART II
THE CREATION OF
THE NEW TITLE I

Improving America's Schools for Children in Greatest Need

by Thomas W. Payzant and Jessica Levin

Thomas W. Payzant is Assistant Secretary for Elementary and Secondary Education in the U.S. Department of Education. He was a teacher and administrator in public schools for more than 30 years. Prior to joining the Clinton Administration in 1993, he served for 10 years as superintendent of the San Diego City Schools.

Jessica Levin is a special assistant to the Under Secretary of the U.S. Department of Education. She has been extensively involved in the reauthorization of the Elementary and Secondary Education Act, particularly the Title I program. Prior to joining the Education Department, she directed the National Chapter 1 Advocacy Project, a nationwide education advocacy initiative based at the Center for Law and Education in Washington, D.C.

The authors wish to thank Mary Jean LeTendre, Director of the Compensatory Education Program in the U.S. Department of Education, for her support and advice. Jonathan Schnur also made invaluable contributions to this essay, and the authors thank him for his time and editing.

Three decades after its creation by the historic Elementary and Secondary Education Act of 1965, the Title I program remains the centerpiece of the federal commitment to elementary and secondary education. In 1965, Title I symbolized a new era of federal involvement in education, with federal assistance focusing on students who needed it most: poor and disadvantaged children. In 1994, the reauthorization of Chapter 1 in the Improving America's Schools Act of 1994 (IASA) signals an important new era in the history of federal education programs.[1]

The reauthorization of Chapter 1 (returning to its original name, Title I) reaffirms the values that have undergirded Title I since its inception: a commitment to equity and to meeting the educational needs of disadvantaged children. However, it adopts dramatically different strategies for addressing those needs.

The new Title I calls for high standards for all children and comprehensive schoolwide reform strategies to enable all children to achieve these standards. It rejects the program's decades-long reliance on isolated, add-on services, as well as the lower expectations for the children it serves. Instead, the new Title I embraces a fundamentally different approach — one that seeks every opportunity to focus Title I dollars on leveraging overall improvement of teaching and learning in schools with the highest levels of poverty.

This new strategy is designed to significantly increase the opportunities of schools, districts, and states to raise the achievement of all children, but particularly those who always have been the intended beneficiaries of Title I — poor children, low-achieving children, migrant children, children who are neglected or at risk of dropping out, and limited-English-proficient children. This strategy reflects the Title I reauthorization proposal submitted by the Clinton Administration to Congress in 1993, as well as a widespread consensus that emerged early in the reauthorization discussions on the critical changes needed in Chapter 1. Moreover, this Title I strategy directly addresses the new realities of a rapidly changing world, not only one in which the nation, schools, and particularly children face increasing challenges, but also wherein knowledge about how to address these challenges and improve teaching and learning has expanded significantly.

The vision and structure of the Title I legislation differs from the old Chapter 1. The new law calls on everyone involved in the program — schools, districts, states, the federal government, communities, parents, and children — to play fundamentally changed roles. The former Chapter 1 frequently fragmented programs and separated people from one another; the new Title I strives to bring people and programs together. It is designed to work with other IASA programs and to reinforce overall reform efforts in schools, districts, and states. It also seeks to redirect the energies and attention of school systems from compliance and process to quality and results. The new law creates important new challenges and responsibilities but also dramatically expands opportunities for using Title I to benefit the nation's children.

The Context for Title I Change

Few reauthorizations have benefited from as much thought and discussion as the 1994 reauthorization of the Chapter 1 law. In fact, consideration of the reauthorization began several years before the Clinton Administration submitted its proposal to Congress. Over that period, both Congress and the Education Department held extensive hearings. Concurrently, several detailed public studies, reports, and recommendations on the program — including the National Assessment of Chapter 1 — were produced and widely disseminated. Several commissions, including the Independent Review Panel of the National Assessment of Chapter 1, the Advisory Committee on Testing in Chapter 1, and, most notably, the Commission on Chapter 1, also provided forums for researchers, policy makers, educators, and advocates to build a powerful consensus for Title I change.

A confluence of critical factors shaped the transformation of the Title I program and provided the basis for this consensus:

1. *A Transforming Society and Economy.* During the past three decades, America has experienced profound societal, economic, and demographic changes that have significantly affected the Title I program. Because these issues are discussed in great depth elsewhere in this book, we will only highlight a few of the most relevant issues here.

Perhaps most significantly, these dramatic changes have meant that the historic, and almost exclusive, focus on basic literacy in Chapter 1 no longer addresses the educational needs of society. Thinking, problem-solving, and decision-making skills that enable a child to work independently, as well as collaboratively, are now essential to finding a good job and becoming a productive member of our democratic society.

In addition, while success requires increasingly high levels of education, the challenges facing America's poorest and most disadvantaged students are greater than ever. In the 1990s, many more children than in past decades are growing up in poverty, in unstable families, and in communities and schools plagued by drugs and violence. Many children face these challenges without the supports they have traditionally received from a variety of societal institutions and their community as a whole. In this context, the roles and responsibilities of families, schools, and other public and private institutions that serve children and youth are increasingly challenging and not always clear. While these changes have affected the entire society, they have had the greatest effect on the very children whose education Title I has been designed to support.

Though these challenges may seem daunting, they have been accompanied by an enormous expansion of knowledge about how to improve teaching and learning to enable all children — including those in poverty — to succeed in this rapidly changing and complex world.

2. *An Expanding Knowledge Base.* Twenty-five years of research have provided us with solid lessons on raising student achievement. Although some of these lessons might seem intuitive, their importance makes them worth repeating.

- All students can learn to much higher levels than we thought in the past. The research is clear: high expectations lead to high achievement, low expectations do not. The expansion in numbers of students taking and passing Advance Placement courses, the success of children in high-poverty schools where exemplary teaching and learning take place, and the increase in the number of students enrolled and succeeding in rigorous algebra and geometry courses all demonstrate this lesson.
- What a child is taught matters. Both the type of subjects a child is taught (for example, whether it is algebra or general math) and the material presented in each subject contribute to higher levels of achievement. Content-rich instruction is indispensable for all children.
- The quality of teaching matters. There is no single best way for teachers to teach and children to learn. Nonetheless, we can determine what works and what fails and use this knowledge to shape instructional practices. For example, we know that engaging students as active learners is a key to successful teaching, but this knowledge is too often ignored.
- Teachers are more likely to teach well what they understand and have been taught to teach. We all have seen the effects of an elementary school teacher's apprehension about science. Good teaching requires both knowledge of subject matter and an understanding of multiple ways to meaningfully engage students in that subject.
- Tests drive what is taught. Too often we fail to test the knowledge all children need to succeed, thereby placing students and teachers alike at a disadvantage and undermining the utility of the assessments as an objective measure of what students know and can do. Assessments aligned with challenging curricula can remove the traditional tension between teaching and testing.
- Schools improve when the people in those schools are invested in and committed to improving teaching and learning. Eliminating the dichotomy between program planning and implementation

can help unite all members of a school community around a common vision of improvement.
- Education reform efforts have a long history in the United States, but their success usually is short-lived because these efforts tend to be narrow and categorical, rather than comprehensive and integrated into the operation of the whole school.

These lessons played a role not only in shaping the new Title I, but the entire IASA reauthorization. They also provide a knowledge base on which we can build a high-quality education system for all students.

3. *Chapter 1 Evaluation Under the Hawkins-Stafford Amendments of 1988.* The reauthorization of the former Chapter 1 law benefited not only from this new knowledge, but also from the findings of several rigorous evaluations on the effectiveness of the Chapter 1 program. These Chapter 1 evaluations, many of them spearheaded by the U.S. Department of Education, demonstrated that despite some real successes throughout the years, the Chapter 1 program was still far from realizing its full potential.

In the 1970s and most of the 1980s, Chapter 1 helped to reduce inequities in public education and to support a national effort to improve the basic skills of all children. During this period, for example, the gap in mathematics achievement between students in disadvantaged urban communities and more advantaged students narrowed substantially, according to the National Assessment of Educational Progress (NAEP).[2]

In more recent years, progress has stalled. Performance data from *Prospects*, a longitudinal assessment of Chapter 1 students' progress, suggested that the Chapter 1 program was no longer closing the gap between disadvantaged children and others.[3] Over a one-year period, for example, Chapter 1 participants did not improve their relative standing in reading or math in the fourth grade or in math in the eighth grade; only eighth-grade reading participants showed improvement relative to their peers. Chapter 1 participants did no better on norm-referenced or criterion-referenced tests than nonparticipants with similar background and prior achievement.

However, these data merely confirmed the lessons derived from our collective experience. Despite the best efforts of policy makers, administrators, and school staff, Chapter 1 programs seldom have triggered the broad changes that are needed in schools to enable all students to meet the high standards demanded in these challenging times. Nor have they met the overall purpose of the 1988 Chapter 1 law, "to improve the educational opportunities of educationally deprived children by helping such children succeed in the regular program of the LEA, attain grade-level proficiency, and improve achievement in basic and more advanced skills."

4. *The Operation of the Former Chapter 1 Program.* Of course, a summary of these findings can mask the important role that Chapter 1 has played in the education of many disadvantaged children. Perhaps most critically, the former Chapter 1 helped to focus the nation's attention on the education needs of disadvantaged children. Until the late 1980s, it also significantly helped to close the gap in basic skills achievement between disadvantaged students and their more advantaged peers. Moreover, Chapter 1 has been at the forefront of efforts to involve parents in all aspects of their children's education and has laid the groundwork for broader parent involvement in education generally.

Many Chapter 1 programs, and those who have worked tirelessly in them, also have made important differences in the education and lives of individual students through such strategies as innovative extended-time opportunities, effective individualized attention, increased professional development opportunities for teachers, and effective coordination of Chapter 1 services with other health and social services.

However, under the former Chapter 1 law, these examples remained isolated success stories, rather than the norm. Key features of the program sometimes worked against success, thereby preventing effective practices from going to scale.

School districts have played the largest role in designing and operating the former Chapter 1 program. The 1988 Chapter 1 law required districts to use their Chapter 1 resources "to meet the special needs of . . . educationally deprived children at the pre-school, elementary and secondary levels." According to the law, this included conducting an "assessment of educational needs" to determine both the grades and children to receive Chapter 1 services and the design of those services to address those children's needs.

However, too often the Chapter 1 program decisions have not reflected the specific needs of either individual schools or students. Typically, districts have decided to conduct a Chapter 1 program in the same grades and subject areas in every school served by Chapter 1. Then they have assigned additional Chapter 1 staff to each school based on its total number of children who score below an established cut-off point on a districtwide test. For example, every 40 Chapter 1 children below this cut-off point may generate one additional Title I teacher and 1.5 Title I teacher aides.

The result has been a district-directed "one-size-fits-all" Chapter 1 program. That "one-size" in 70% of Chapter 1 schools has been the Chapter 1 "pull-out" program.[4] These pull-out programs, by and large, have taken children identified for Chapter 1 out of their regular classrooms during prime class time for instruction in a separate location. Chapter 1 staff have provided this instruction, often through "drill and practice" on basic reading and math skills. Although pull-out programs have replaced a student's regular class period, research shows that, on average, they have added only 10 minutes of extra instruction a day.[5] Therefore, participation in pull-out programs has come with a high price tag for children — missing the regular instructional program. Moreover, even the best Chapter 1 pull-out programs have had little effect on the regular program of instruction, where the children served by Chapter 1 still spend most of their school day.

To address this latter problem, the 1988 reauthorization of Chapter 1 expanded the opportunities for schools to develop schoolwide projects — permitting any school with more than 75% poverty to use Chapter 1 funds to serve all children in a school and "to upgrade the entire educational program," rather than to provide "add-on" services for identified children. But even where schoolwide projects have reduced class size, they rarely have stimulated the additional instructional reforms needed to enable all students to improve achievement.

The jobs of teachers, administrators, and parents also have been complicated by the absence of an overall framework and clear goals to guide their efforts. Rather, the program has been driven by federally mandated, norm-referenced tests and the watered-down goal of minimum achievement gains on these tests. This has reinforced Chapter 1's low expectations and heavy reliance on drill and practice.

Despite codifying these low expectations, the program improvement provisions of the former Chapter 1 law did significantly advance Chapter 1 accountability by beginning to focus on achievement gains, rather than just on compliance with prescribed procedures. For the first time, the law outlined a consequence for schools failing to make progress: identification for "program improvement." Nonetheless, schools did not receive the professional development and support they needed to significantly improve their programs.

Although Chapter 1 is the largest federal education program (funded at $6.7 billion in the 1994-95 school year), it is still only one of many federal, state, and local programs serving the nation's students. In fact, the typical high-poverty urban elementary school may have as many as 15 or 20 unconnected programs, each with its own staff, plan, evaluation, and reporting requirements. These programs, taken together, are extraordinarily difficult to administer and absorb considerable energy from all involved. They also inhibit a sense of ownership and responsibility among school staff for the education of each child. It is all too common to hear, "Chapter 1 children are not my responsibility; they are the responsibility of the Chapter 1 teacher." "Limited-English-proficient children? They belong in that other classroom, not mine."

These conclusions do not negate Chapter 1's successes. Nor are they meant to cast any blame on those who have been working hard to achieve what they thought would be in the best interest of children. But the implications are clear: the former Chapter 1 program cannot adequately address the needs of children in the changing context of the 1990s.

Converting Title I into an Important Tool to Enable All Children to Achieve High Standards

Early in the reauthorization, there was widespread agreement about the need for a significant overhaul of the former Chapter 1 law and the importance of converting the program into a more effective tool for those working in Title I schools to help students reach high standards. There also was remarkable consensus on the major new strategies that the new Title I should embrace: 1) a focus on teaching and learning, 2) comprehensive schoolwide reform strategies, 3) greater program flexibility, 4) targeting of resources, and 5) new partnerships to address the full range of children's needs affecting their ability to learn.

However, Title I was not the first federal law to benefit from this new consensus. The Goals 2000: Educate America Act[6] — the Clinton Administration's education initiative to support overall state and local school reform efforts — first embraced these principles with broad bipartisan support. The Goals 2000 Act also provided a critical framework for how Title I, the rest of the IASA, and other education programs could work together to support overall state and local reforms to improve student achievement. This helped lay additional groundwork for the fundamental changes in the new Title I law.

New Goal — Helping All Children Reach High Standards. The emphasis on high standards for all children provides a clearly defined goal for the new Title I law: enabling children served by the program to achieve to the challenging standards established by the state. In fact, the new Title I makes a powerful break with past practice by replacing minimum standards for some children with challenging standards for all. Challenging state content standards become the centerpiece of the new Title I law.

But asking for high standards will not guarantee getting them. The history of the Title I/Chapter 1 program offers a different lesson. Any separate system of standards and assessments for Title I is likely to be a system with lower standards. Therefore, the standards and assessments used for Title I purposes must be the same as those used by the state for all its other students, either under Goals 2000 or any other statewide process. Only in the absence of overall standards and assessments for all children will states develop standards and assessments just for Title I.

In addition to supporting higher expectations for children in Title I schools, challenging content standards — defining what all children should know and be able to do — can provide a substantive framework so sorely needed in the Title I program. Under this framework, all aspects of the education system — high-quality assessments, curriculum and instruction, professional development, school leadership, and school improvement — can work together to ensure that all children served by Title I achieve high standards. Moreover, the standards can support a stronger results-based accountability system, in which the success of the system is measured according to how well all its parts help students meet the standards. As a result, under the new Title I, high standards replace federally mandated, low-level, norm-referenced tests as the driving force behind education change.

Focusing on Teaching and Learning. Research suggests that for all students to achieve to high standards, states, districts, and schools must maintain a constant focus on improving teaching and learning. For far too long, teaching and learning played a subordinate role to administration, process, and compliance with rules and regulations in the Chapter 1 program.

Thus the first major reform strategy in the new Title I is moving teaching and learning to center stage. Everything we do ought to be guided by this fundamental question: What difference do what I decide and what I do make for teaching and learning? If this question cannot be answered for a particular Title I decision — whether about priorities, allocation of resources, or institutional practices — that decision is unlikely to make a positive difference for children.

Asking this question will lead to a new focus on what children are taught and how they are taught. This will likely mean replacing remediation with an accelerated curriculum and replacing drill and practice with more enriched instruction. It also will require a greater reliance on proven practices, rather than the latest fads. And it means that schools that continue to target resources on their lowest-achieving children must explore ways other than traditional pull-out programs, such as extended time strategies (extended day or extended year programs) that build on a challenging regular program for all children.

A focus on teaching and learning also necessitates a new investment and approach to professional development, recognizing that teachers, like the students they teach, are continuous learners. This new professional development — intensive, sustained, and embedded in the daily lives of teachers — will prove critical to helping teachers understand and teach to high standards. Therefore, Title I and Title II of the Improving America's Schools Act strongly reinforce each other through this new focus on teaching and learning.

Promoting Comprehensive, Schoolwide Reform to Improve Teaching and Learning. Evaluations of the former Chapter 1 program, as well as three decades of experience with pull-out programs, have demonstrated that the program's structure prevented it from sufficiently supporting improvements in teaching and learning. The development, under the former law, of "in-class" Chapter 1 programs — where Chapter 1 staff provide additional help to Chapter 1 students within the regular classroom — was one response to the widespread criticism of pull-out programs. However, unless in-class programs also are carefully structured to minimize the segregation of Chapter 1 children in the classroom, they can perpetuate the tracking, stigmatization, and fragmentation commonly found in pull-out programs.

Therefore the new Title I law embraces a radically different strategy: comprehensive school reform through schoolwide programs. It embodies the adage that "a rising tide lifts all boats." This reflects the belief that a strategy for total school improvement can more effectively lift the achievement levels of all children, including those who are farthest behind, as long as schools understand their responsibility to serve every child and to expect every child to learn. Moreover, schoolwide approaches can help bring entire school staffs together to develop and implement comprehensive plans for improving teaching and learning for all students, eliminating the isolation that characterizes working conditions for so many educators.

In support of this new approach, the new Title I significantly expands the ability of schools to develop schoolwide programs by lowering the minimum poverty level eligibility from 75% to 60% poor children in school year 1995-1996, and to 50% percent poverty in subsequent years. While there still will be some schools — called targeted assistance schools — that must continue to direct their Title I resources to their lowest achieving students, there will be 12,000 more schools (for a total of 20,000 schools nationwide) that will be able to use Title I funds to "upgrade the entire educational program" in the school.

We emphasize that this shift in Title I diminishes neither the program's continuing commitment to equity nor its central purpose of meeting the educational needs of disadvantaged children. Indeed, it is the strength of this commitment that has led to a dramatically new program approach for addressing those needs.

Freeing Schools, Districts, and States to Better Enable Reforms. Launching comprehensive reform efforts to support schoolwide improvements in teaching and learning will require far more time, energy, and latitude than currently are available to most Title I schools. Differing requirements, conflicting planning provisions, and separate accountability mechanisms associated with different program funds can further complicate their best efforts to launch and sustain comprehensive reforms.

Recognizing this, Title I strives to give schoolwide programs greater flexibility and more opportunities than they had under the former law. Under the new law, a schoolwide program will not have to draw solely on its Title I funds. Instead, a school may use the vast majority of all of its federal funds, as well as its state and local funds, to support the schoolwide program. In addition, schoolwide programs no longer will have to conform to the specific statutory and regulatory provisions of each separate federal program as long as the intent and purposes of those programs, as well as certain requirements relating to such critical areas as civil rights and health and safety, are met. No longer should there be "Title I schoolwides" or even "IASA schoolwides," but simply a single schoolwide program, supported by a school's resources.

Other new vehicles to support increased flexibility in Title I include: greater school-level decision making for all schoolwide and targeted assistance schools; the opportunity for states and districts to develop a single consolidated plan, rather than separate plans, for all of their IASA programs; and the unprecedented ability of states, districts, and schools to seek waivers of provisions in the Title I law that impede their efforts to support higher student achievement.

Channeling More Title I Resources to High-Poverty Schools. Greater concentration of Title I funds can better leverage comprehensive reforms in schoolwide programs and support higher quality programs in all Title I schools. For this reason and on grounds of fundamental fairness, the Clinton Administration sought to better channel Title I resources to areas where the needs were greatest.

While this overall goal was only partially achieved by the reauthorization, several new Title I provisions promise to channel more funds to high-poverty schools in every school district. First, districts will allocate funds to every Title I school based on its total number of poor children, rather than the number of low-achieving children. This not only will bring more funds to the highest poverty schools but also will eliminate existing penalties for success. Second, districts that serve any school below 35% poverty must allocate a minimum number of dollars per child to all schools that it serves. Third, tightened eligibility rules will allow districts to serve schools below the district poverty average only if the school has a poverty rate of 35% or more. Finally, in order to ensure that Title I resources flow to the most needy middle and high schools, districts must serve *all* schools with poverty rates above 75% before serving any other school.

The new Title I ensures more effective use of Title I funds, not only through a greater concentration of those funds in high-poverty schools, but also by establishing clear strategic priorities for their use throughout the education system.

Bringing Schools, Families, and Communities Together to Address Other Needs that Affect Learning. The final, major Title I strategy involves bringing schools, families, and communities together to address the wide array of other needs that affect a child's learning. We all know that other factors in the lives of children — poor health, inadequate nutrition, family problems, violence — significantly affect their ability to learn.

Schools cannot do everything alone, particularly as they redouble their efforts to improve teaching and learning. Therefore, the new Title I calls on parents to take advantage of a wide range of new opportunities to support their children's learning. Moreover, schools and their districts are called on to engage parents, community members, business people, and other agencies that serve children and families as partners in supporting the success of children. The entire IASA, in fact, is built on the premise that broad partnerships are necessary to provide comprehensive support for children so that good teaching and learning *can* take place in all schools.

Forging an Integrated Education System. To accomplish its goal of enabling all children to achieve high standards, the new Title I law attempts to convert the program from a separate set of services into a critical support for schools, districts, and states as they implement overall reforms. In fact, all other IASA resources — including professional development resources under Title II, grants for technology to improve teaching and learning under Title III, and additional programs under Title IV to ensure that schools will be safe and drug free — are designed to work with the Title I program to play this important supporting role.

Through its investment in such critical areas as professional development, high-quality instruction, parent involvement, and stronger, results-based reforms, the new Title I law strives to leverage comprehensive new reforms as well as to ensure that reforms already under way become reality. In this context, we no longer can view the Title I program apart from other education programs. Indeed, its success depends on connecting with and supporting all efforts that are designed to enable all children to reach high standards.

New Roles to Take Advantage of New Opportunities

Taken together, all these strategies offer dramatically expanded opportunities to help ensure that all children — whether poor, low-achieving, migrant, LEP, disabled, or gifted — receive the education they need to achieve the high state standards. To take advantage of these strategies, those involved in education — schools, districts, states, the federal government, parents, and children — will have to play fundamentally new roles and work together in new ways to improve teaching and learning.

The School Level — the New Centerpiece of Title I. At the heart of these strategies is a new focus on schools as active and central participants in all aspects of the Title I program. All Title I schools will have far greater authority to make program decisions. This includes deciding whether to develop a schoolwide program, determining how to use the Title I funds to best address the needs of their students, and participating in the selection of the children to be served by a targeted assistance program.

Far greater authority to make decisions will mean that all schools will play a very different role in the new Title I program. Under the former Chapter 1, schools traditionally were on the receiving end of rules and regulations developed by the district and state, with little control over most decisions affecting the design and operation of their programs. Under the new law, schools are far more able to design their own innovative solutions to address their schools' specific problems and needs. Decisions no longer will be made by consulting rules, but by teachers, principals, parents, and other school and district staff consulting one another to determine how a particular decision will promote high-quality teaching and learning.

However, greater latitude does not mean that just anything goes. All schools — schoolwide and targeted assistance schools — must invest in those areas that research suggests are critical to effective reform, including: curriculum, instruction, the quality of program staff, professional development, parental involvement, new partnerships, and accountability for results. But each school can decide, in consultation with its district, how best to channel these investments into improving its Title I program and the achievement of its students.

To be successful, these efforts will require not only unprecedented collaboration but also very different approaches to planning. Too often, school planning has amounted to little more than a compilation of subcommittee reports, each filed behind a separator in a three-ring binder, to be pulled off the shelf when the district requires its resubmission. To free schools to concentrate their planning on their own needs, Title I no longer requires schools to develop plans on a pre-determined cycle nor to submit them to their district or state in order to receive program funds. Instead, schools are encouraged to convert their plans into evolving strategic documents that can be used to marshal a school's resources.

Effective collaboration in support of improved teaching and learning depends on more than just good planning. It also requires every member of the school community to share a sense of responsibility for the success of every student. Moreover, because creativity and personal commitment is so critical to Title I reform, each individual in the school community also will need to explore ways to best tap his or her unique contributions to promote the well-being and the achievement of children. For example, a principal who feels responsible for all students in the school will serve not only as a final arbiter and administrator but also as a facilitator, coach, and advocate who is willing to work closely with all staff and parents to improve the entire school. Teachers and other staff who feel responsible for the success of the school's students will work continually to expand their knowledge about teaching and learning, update their teaching skills, and employ a variety of approaches to actively engage all students in learning. They also will seek new approaches to coordinating instruction with other teachers throughout the school and new ways of effectively involving parents in the education of their children.

Finally, parents have new responsibilities or, more accurately, shared responsibilities with teachers and other school staff. They will be encouraged to join the educators in new Title I compacts, identifying their mutual responsibilities and sustaining an ongoing dialogue about their children's achievement. Many parents also may choose to become involved in the development of overall school policies, including the development of strategies to involve other parents effectively in their children's education. Schools and communities must ensure that parents have the information, training, and other supports they may need to effectively play these roles.

Districts as Facilitators of Title I Change. In order for schools to move successfully to the center stage of Title I reform, they must receive far greater training and technical assistance. The new law calls on school districts to forgo making some of their traditional decisions and instead take on this support role in at least four critical ways.

First, school districts will be called on to work with schools as they develop their Title I programs and to ensure that schools receive any technical assistance needed for effective program implementation. This support could involve drawing on the district's own expertise for school planning efforts or providing schools with an opportunity to learn about what works in other schools. A major source of support also may include connecting schools to other technical assistance providers, such as universities, regional labs, and the new IASA technical assistance centers.

Second, a district will work with school-level staff to develop a strategy for improved professional development, equipping all teachers and other staff who are involved in the education of the children served by the Title I program to teach to high standards. A one-hour presentation on "everything you need to know about the new math curriculum" at the end of a full day of teaching is no longer enough. Instead, ongoing, high-quality professional development funded by Title I should be connected to overall school improvement strategies and classroom practice and, where possible, integrated into teachers' daily work. This can include significant regular planning time and ongoing opportunities for teachers to learn from their successful colleagues.

Third, under the new Title I law, school districts will play a critical role in helping to forge greater connections among schools and between schools, communities, and other social agencies. Although schools, particularly high-poverty ones, can benefit greatly from such connections, they often have trouble creating them. Therefore, the new

Title I asks each district to coordinate the Title I program with other education programs and, to the extent feasible, with services provided by other agencies that serve children and families. This includes providing for the sufficient transition of young children from Head Start and other preschool programs to schools, coordinating family literacy programs and other districtwide parental involvement activities, and, where desired, using up to 5% of its IASA funds for coordination/collaboration activities.

Finally, while it will be critical for districts to support schools as they engage in reforms, districts also will be responsible for holding schools accountable for results. This includes recognizing and rewarding schools that are making satisfactory progress on a regular basis and identifying for "school improvement" those schools that do not make such progress for two consecutive years. It also requires districts to ensure that schools failing to make adequate progress first receive the technical assistance they need but, ultimately, face corrective actions for persistently low performance.

Taking these responsibilities seriously will require the district to shift its focus from compliance to quality and from "command and control" to "suggest and support." It will call on district staff members to draw heavily on their own knowledge of teaching, learning, and organizational change. Whether schools succeed in their new Title I roles will depend in part on how well districts carry out their own new Title I responsibilities.

Anchoring the Program: State Standards and Assessments. Each state also has a new, critical role to play under the new Title I law. That is providing an anchor and framework to support the new Title I program. At the core of this framework will be high-quality, challenging standards and assessments that are created by the states, not mandated by the federal government. States will be able to develop their own content and performance standards and high-quality, carefully aligned assessments to determine how well children are meeting those standards. States also can approve the use of district-adopted standards and aligned assessments for Title I purposes — but only if those standards and assessments are at least as challenging as the state's and meet the other requirements of the law.

Each state will anchor the Title I accountability system through its definition of yearly "adequate progress" in meeting state standards for districts and schools. Adequate progress will provide the basis for identifying schools and districts for improvement and must be defined with sufficient rigor to enable all children to meet the state standards.

Other state responsibilities for ensuring Title I accountability and improvement include holding districts responsible for their own performance through mechanisms similar to those established for schools and supplementing other available support to both schools and their districts through such mechanisms as school support teams and distinguished educators.

Also, each state will play a critical role in ensuring that education programs can work together to support systemic reform efforts. In fact, the success of systemic reform depends on the ability of the state to help all education programs work together to support an overall vision for reform and improved student achievement. Some key strategies to link Title I with other programs, and an overall reform effort, include the use of state standards and assessments for Title I purposes, the design of Title I programs to support overall reform efforts, and the use of Title I resources to ensure that children in low-income schools and districts benefit from these efforts. With its unique perspective, the state can help maximize the benefits not just of Title I, but of all federal, state, and local education programs.

The Federal Role — Forging a New Partnership for Title I Change. Because the federal government plays such a critical role in shaping the Title I program at all other levels, the federal government also must play a dramatically new Title I role. The federal government has long been the source of Title I's command-and-control approach, supplying plenty of mandates about the operation of Title I programs but little extra support to enhance program effectiveness. The new Title I is designed to promote a different federal approach that relies on assistance, rather than solely on enforcement, and program support, rather than program control.

For example, the federal government no longer will require federally mandated tests for the Title I program. Schools will be more able to draw on their federal funds to support comprehensive reforms that meet their needs. Fifteen comprehensive technical centers also will bring the expertise of the former categorical program centers together to make it easier for states, districts, and schools to benefit from these sources of expertise. This "one-stop shopping" will be particularly helpful to the growing number of schools, districts, and states engaged in comprehensive reform.

Meanwhile, the Department of Education's implementation strategies are designed to further revamp the federal role in Title I. The department is working to enable states, districts, and schools to take full advantage of the new flexibility in the law. Regulations will be avoided wherever possible and, when used, will seek to expand rather than curtail options. The department's plan to integrate its monitoring across programs and to focus increasingly on quality and results will further redefine how it relates to states, districts, and schools.

This new federal approach under the IASA is part of the Clinton Administration's broad education reform strategy of moving programmatic decisions to states, districts, and schools, with far less prescription from Washington; redirecting the energies of entire school systems from compliance and enforcement to support, technical assistance, peer review, and continuous improvement; and forging a new federal, state, and local partnership that reflects education as a national priority and a state and local responsibility.

Challenges and Opportunities

In the wake of most reauthorizations, many schools, districts, and states ask, What new rules have you created for us to follow? Under the dramatically new approach in the Title I law, schools, districts, and states will not have new rules to follow but new roles to play. These new roles provide exciting opportunities for those involved in Title I and in education generally. But reaping their benefit will require a fundamental transformation in approaches, attitudes, and culture throughout our education system. We will briefly describe four of the most significant challenges involved in this transformation.

The Challenge of Improving Teaching and Learning. The first, and perhaps the most significant, challenge will involve shifting the Title I program focus to improving teaching and learning and ensuring that all those who work in schools, districts, and states are equipped to make this important change. Focusing on improving teaching and learning represents a dramatic change from the traditional focus of Chapter 1/ Title I on compliance with uniform solutions. Asking schools to comply with rules and regulations, established far from where teaching and learning take place, may promote a comforting uniformity, but this approach does not provide a solid foundation for a responsive education system in which teachers and other staff determine how best to meet the education needs of their students.

However, making such decisions, particularly when they involve deliberations with all members of the school community, may seem far more difficult for schools than merely identifying the right person to answer specific questions. This shift also may present important challenges to program staff and administrators at all levels. Instead of their tried-and-true role of setting and enforcing rules, they now must explore how best to support teachers and other staff to improve teaching and learning. This challenge may be increased because of the potential unwillingness of some individuals to take risks amid uncertainty about how others in the system will react.

In addition, despite the dramatic increase in our knowledge about how to improve teaching and learning, there still are no pat answers. Therefore, all members of a school system will need to draw far more extensively on their skills as professionals. The ability of educators to meet this challenge will depend on their willingness to invest time and energy in examining how everything in an education system affects teaching and learning and in continuing to develop their own skills. The new Title I law is designed to support all those working to meet this challenge.

Shifting the Title I Paradigm from Separate Programs to Comprehensive School Reforms. The second challenge is setting in motion reform efforts at all levels that are both comprehensive and coherent and that address the needs of the most disadvantaged children. For three decades, the Title I law has served disadvantaged children by identifying them and targeting additional services to meet their specific needs. The new Title I shifts the paradigm, promoting comprehensive schoolwide approaches to raise the achievement of all children in high-poverty schools, rather than providing separate add-on programs that merely supplement the regular instruction for the lowest-achieving children.

Significant discussions took place during the reauthorization about the implications of this more comprehensive approach. For example, some participants were concerned that if the funds of other targeted federal programs were included in schoolwide programs, the needs of their targeted populations would be neglected. Others wanted to ensure that using statewide assessments for Title I purposes would not reduce the availability of information about specific groups of children and accountability for their results. Faced with these concerns, Congress did add several additional requirements affecting Title I schoolwide programs and assessments. But the new Title I still emerged from these discussions with a strong commitment to comprehensive schoolwide reform and to one system of standards and assessments for all children.

Nonetheless, issues concerning comprehensive reform and meeting the needs of specific children likely will continue to present challenges for those working to implement the new law. These challenges can be better met if a school community views the education of all students as a shared responsibility and collaborates in designing and implementing comprehensive strategies that meet the needs of all children.

Forging Meaningful Accountability. Third, meaningful accountability must be fostered, whereby people are responsible for the consequences of their work and have a sense of personal accountability for how their actions affect student achievement.

The new Title I will make significant strides toward building a more effective accountability system through its call for high standards, aligned assessments, and consequences for both success and failure. If schools, districts, and states are willing to set challenging standards and impose real consequences for success and failure, this form of accountability can play an important role in school improvement.

Still more is needed. We must continue to make strides toward a more effective, responsive form of accountability, where all stakeholders, but particularly those closest to children — teachers and parents — will have the information and ability to correct, modify, and improve their work on an ongoing basis. While a system of rewards and penalties for success and failure is important, its effect is far more blunt and transient than motivating everyone involved in education to hold themselves, and each other, accountable for how well they are helping students every day.

The new Title I law is designed to foster this latter form of accountability through such mechanisms as clear and high standards, ongoing information about school and student performance, professional development and technical assistance, greater school-level decision making, and strong parent involvement. But there is one more critical ingredient of this new accountability that no law can mandate. That is a sense of personal and professional responsibility felt by each member of the school community for his or her own effectiveness and the achievement of children. Herein lies the greatest challenge to real accountability in education.

Long-term Strategies for Sustained Educational Reform. All members of the school community, the education system, and the public must be prepared to make a commitment to education for the long haul. Experience and research, not to mention common sense, confirm that there are no quick fixes in education. Too often people in this society expect that a short-term investment in education will yield a quick payoff, and they are likely to withdraw their interest and support if short-term gains are not realized. But just as any parent knows that raising a child takes a lifetime of effort, so does developing and sustaining an education system that provides real educational opportunities for all students.

None of the Clinton Administration initiatives — Goals 2000, IASA, School-to-Work — are quick fixes. They provide important support for cohesive, thoughtful, and long-term strategies for improving teaching and learning across our nation. Persistence, continuity, and hard work — all over the long-term — will be critical to realizing the full potential of our investments.

Whether we succeed or fail with the new Title I will make a world of difference. For high-poverty schools, it will mean the difference between participating fully in promising reform efforts in their states and school districts or remaining on the sidelines as these efforts proceed. And for the neediest children, it will mean the difference between finding doors opened or closed to them when they are adults — doors to high-wage jobs, doors to participation in our democratic society, doors to personal fulfillment, and doors to quality lives.

Footnotes

1. The Improving America's Schools Act of 1994, Public Law 103-382, amended the Elementary and Secondary Education Act of 1965 (ESEA). Title I of the ESEA reauthorizes, for a five-year period, programs currently under Chapter 1 of Title I of the ESEA.
2. U.S. Department of Education, Office of Policy and Planning, Planning and Evaluation Service, *Reinventing Chapter 1: The Current Chapter 1 Program and New Directions, Final Report of the National Assessment of Chapter 1* (Washington, D.C., February 1993), pp. 62, 216.
3. Abt Associates, "Prospects: The Congressionally Mandated Study of Educational Growth and Opportunity," May 1993. Cited in U.S. Department of Education, Office of Policy and Planning, Planning and Evaluation Service, *Reinventing Chapter 1: The Current Chapter 1 Program and New Directions, Final Report of the National Assessment of Chapter 1* (Washington, D.C., February 1993), pp. 99-104.
4. U.S. Department of Education, Office of Policy and Planning, Planning and Evaluation Service, *Reinventing Chapter 1: The Current Chapter 1 Program and New Directions, Final Report of the National Assessment of Chapter 1* (Washington, D.C., February 1993), pp. 79-80.
5. Ibid., p. 82.
6. The Goals 2000: Educate America Act, Public Law 103-227.

Making Schools Work for Children in Poverty

By Kati Haycock and David Hornbeck

Kati Haycock is the director of the Education Trust at the American Association for Higher Education. Established in 1992, the Education Trust assists school districts and institutions of higher education to launch simultaneous reform efforts aimed at improving teaching and learning, especially for minority and low-income students. The Education Trust also provides policy leadership at the national level.

David Hornbeck is superintendent of schools for the Philadelphia public school district. He was one of the architects of the legislation that restructured public education in Kentucky. He has served as an education advisor to the New American Schools Development Corporation, the Center for the Study of Social Policy, and the Business Roundtable. He also was the director of the Washington-based National Alliance for Restructuring Education prior to accepting the Philadelphia superintendency.

In December 1990, a group of 28 leading educators, child advocates, business executives, and local school officials came together to form an independent Commission on Chapter 1. Our goal was to identify ways to increase the effectiveness of the $7 billion federal Chapter 1 program in improving outcomes for poor children, especially those attending schools with concentrations of students from low-income families.

From the beginning, it seemed clear to us that dramatically improved results would require a major shift in the way educators — and Americans generally — think about education for poor children. In those early months, though, few of us who had agreed to serve as commissioners dared even to imagine that we would succeed in launching such a shift with a transformation of Chapter 1. After all, with assistance from overprotective advocates and a politically active bureaucracy, the 27-year-old program had managed to escape serious reform throughout its history. Moreover, the Administration that was then (and seemed likely to remain) in power had shown no interest in taking on the tough political task of Chapter 1 reform.

But four years, one report, and countless hours of sweat later, President Clinton signed into law the Improving America's Schools Act (IASA). That law contains a new Title I that is rooted in the Commission's proposals.

Background

During its 28-year history, Chapter 1/Title I was reauthorized eight times. In each of these reauthorizations, Congress found problems to be fixed. In the early days, those problems were related mostly to financial abuses. In the 1988 reauthorization, the perceived problems centered on the overwhelming focus on low-level skills and the lack of accountability for student achievement. However, for the most part Congress was content with this Great Society program, and members used the reauthorization process to expand the size of the program and to make minor repairs.

Washington-based advocacy organizations also were content throughout the 1970s and 1980s to leave the program as it was. Most saw it as primarily a vehicle to get federal dollars to resource-starved school districts. And so they were more interested in the *formula* than in any other aspect of the legislation. In fact, advocacy groups continuously described Chapter 1 as a "proven" federal program, suggesting that its only problem was that it was not "fully funded."

In truth, there were deeper problems with Chapter 1. Thus, in late 1989, a small group of advocates and foundation executives agreed to put together an independent commission to take a closer look at the program and to make recommendations about how it could be improved. David Hornbeck, a former Maryland state superintendent of schools and then consultant for the Business Roundtable and the National Center for Education and the Economy, agreed to serve as chair. (See full list of commission members on page 88.)

All of the individuals chosen for the commission had long experience with the education of poor and minority children. Indeed, among them, the commissioners had a total of 670 years of experience. All of the commissioners also had been vigorous in their support for the Chapter 1 program and believed that it had contributed significantly to achievement gains among poor children over the past two decades. But we agreed to take the difficult step of conducting a thorough re-examination of the program because of growing evidence that, whatever its contributions in the past, Chapter 1 was inadequate to meet the challenges of the 1990s and beyond.

How the Commission Worked

Support from two foundations made it possible for us to come together on a bimonthly basis over two years to review problems in the program and discuss possible solutions. Staff assistance was provided by the resource center at the Council of Chief State School Officers, which provided a home for the commission during its first two years, and by legal counsel.

In its early meetings, the commission quickly came to consensus that its work should be founded on the conviction that virtually all children can learn at high levels. We believed that low performance among poor children often was attributable to low standards and expectations, which actually were encouraged by the then-current law. The challenge, the commissioners decided, was to convert Chapter 1 from a law designed to help teach low-level "basic skills" to poor children to one dedicated to spurring the kinds of education change that would result in children born into poverty acquiring the high-level knowledge and skills they would need to succeed in college and careers, as well as to participate fully in the public life of our nation.

As our discussions proceeded, it became clear to the commission that this challenge would not be met simply by making cosmetic changes in Chapter 1. Fundamental changes were necessary in the way whole school systems operate.

The needs for such reform could have been articulated in compelling rhetoric, which is the usual way in which reports from independent commissions are written. But questions would remain. Are the reforms practical? Can they be made to work together to achieve the desired objectives? What are the trade-offs in framing the requirements of the law in different ways?

We decided that the only way to answer these questions and put our ideas to the test was to subject ourselves to the discipline that members of Congress must undergo in drafting specific legislative language. What that meant, practically speaking, is that the commission agreed on an eight-part framework for its proposal, each section of which was discussed at an initial meeting. Counsel to the commission then drafted that section and submitted it for commission review.

Beginning in June 1991, each of the sections of the statutory framework went through several drafts, in some cases as many as seven or eight. As commissioners focused on specific provisions, questions arose as to how they would actually work — by themselves or in conjunction with other provisions — and whether the conclusions and courses of action contained in the framework were based on the best available evidence. The process produced new insights and new changes at every review.

Commission Findings and Recommendations

After two years of study and drafting, the commission completed its report, *Making Schools Work for Children in Poverty.* In the report, the commission described critical problems in the Chapter 1 program, including:

- A continued focus on remediation that denies the richness of learning to those who need more, not less, of what makes education engaging and exciting;
- So much focus on accounting for dollars that attention is deflected from results;
- Resources spread too thinly to make a difference in the neediest schools;
- Methods for evaluating progress that are antiquated (and downright harmful); and
- A perverse incentive structure that discourages schools from working hard to improve student performance.

"But," said the commission, "the core problem with Chapter 1 is even more basic: its 'add-on' design, wherein eligible students get extra help to succeed in the regular school program, cannot work when the regular school program itself is seriously deficient."

Consequently, the commission proposed an entirely new policy framework that sought to transform Chapter 1 from an add-on remedial program to a vehicle for improving whole schools serving concentrations of poor children.

The commission proposed eight strategies:

1. Clear, high standards for what students should know and be able to do;
2. New systems to assess progress toward the standards;
3. Informing parents on how well their children are progressing and how they can help;

4. Investing heavily in the development of teachers, principals, and other adults in the school;
5. Matching funding to need and ensuring equity;
6. Replacing accounting for dollars with accountability for results;
7. Integrating health and social service support; and
8. Rewarding schools that make progress and changing those that do not.

Together, these eight strategies could begin to transform Chapter 1 into an engine for improving schools serving poor children. But each was essential.

The Commission Report and Public Education

The commission's report was released at a press conference in December 1992. The response — from both the press and educators across the country — was immediate. Nearly all of the major dailies covered the release, including several with strong editorial support. The Education Trust at the American Association for Higher Education, which provided a home and staff support for the commission during a second, "public education" phase of its work, was deluged with requests for copies. Staff at the Education Trust eventually distributed more than 30,000 copies of the report. The report also was reprinted in full in *Education Week,* the *AAHE Bulletin,* and *Basic Education.*

During the months following release of its report, the commission mounted a public education effort to share its ideas about the education of poor children with teachers, administrators, parents, community leaders, and newspaper writers across the country. The point was to get people thinking and talking about the education of poor children.

We knew in advance that many of the ideas in *Making Schools Work for Children in Poverty* would be new and rather frightening to many in the traditional Chapter 1 community, including both those who were employed in the program and policy makers associated with the program. After all, 28 years of thinking in remedial terms makes it hard to comprehend all this talk about high standards. But our experiences in carrying the commission's message to *other* local educators were in some ways even more sobering than the interactions with Chapter 1 employees. Many, we discovered, had never even heard of "standards" or "systemic reform."

Therefore, most of our briefings became vehicles to get local educators and community members to think about standards-based reform and what it might mean for poor children in their community. In place of the longer briefings we initially had planned, we organized day-long "mini-institutes," where participants heard from two or three commissioners, listened while some of their peers discussed their reactions, and then worked through some of the issues in small groups. We also sponsored evening sessions for parents and community leaders.

Many of these briefings were held on college campuses and arranged in partnership with local school districts and community organizations. Wherever possible, we tried to make sure that there were mechanisms to keep the discussions going over a period of time. This worked especially well in cities where the Education Trust already had established relationships with local educators.

Participants in these briefings and institutes were invited to become part of a "Chapter 1 Reform Network" after they had a chance to review the commission's recommendations in some detail. The members of this network received updates on the progress of the legislation through Congress.

In addition to local and regional briefings, and much assistance to local educators in understanding this thing called "systemic reform," the commission also provided extensive briefings for the congressional committees charged with reauthorizing elementary and secondary programs in the 1993-94 session. On the House side, we sponsored six such briefings, each focused on exploring one major area of need, including the commission's recommendations in that area and a variety of alternative approaches. On the Senate side, there were three such briefings. The commission also conducted numerous briefings for others in the Washington policy community and shared ideas and information with the new Administration. All of this activity was coordinated by the commission steering committee, which met weekly during the reauthorization process.

The Bill in Congress

Education Secretary Richard Riley sent his proposal for reauthorization of the elementary and secondary programs to the House in September 1993. In the proposed new Title I (a shift back to the original name of the Chapter 1 program), the Administration adopted many of the commission's suggestions. Indeed, much of the architecture for the Education Department's proposal was drawn from suggestions in the commission's report and the report of the Independent Review Panel (which had several members in common with the commission).

The Administration's proposal contained a number of critically important provisions:

- A requirement that states set high standards for all children and develop better tools for assessing progress toward standards;
- Increased concentration of dollars in schools where the need is greatest, and the elimination of "reverse incentives" in current law that take money away from schools that increase student achievement;
- A requirement that holds schools accountable for getting increased numbers of their students to state standards and insists on corrective action for schools that do not make progress; and
- Elimination of the major obstacle in current law to serving limited-English-proficient students and increased coordination with health and social services.

All of these ideas were included in the commission's recommendations, and several also were embraced in the report from the congressionally mandated Independent Review Panel.

Some observers have suggested that the commission simply "got lucky" when two commissioners, Marshall Smith and Sharon Robinson, were appointed as Under Secretary and Assistant Secretary of Education. We prefer to think of it not as luck, but as good planning. Regardless, former commissioner and current Under Secretary Smith did indeed play the lead role in the Education Department in shaping Secretary Riley's proposal, and we assume that his participation on the commission helped to gel his ideas about reform of Chapter 1.

But in spite of the general tenor of the proposal, commissioners believed that there were critical deficiencies in the Administration's proposal. These deficiencies, taken together, substantially undermined the goal of reinventing Chapter 1. The critical deficiencies included:

- The accountability provisions did not insist on — or even report — results for disadvantaged groups of students.
- Though the floor for schoolwide use of Title I money was lowered to 50% poverty, in at least half of schools receiving these funds, Title I would remain an add-on program; and such schools would not be pressed to improve instruction in the school as a whole.
- Schools serving poor children had no guaranteed funding to support the high-quality professional and organizational development they need to get their students to high standards.
- States were not encouraged or required to take even minimal steps to reduce disparities within their borders in the educational resources invested in students who live in different communities, or otherwise to ensure that poor districts had the wherewithal to get their students to high standards.

Commission chair David Hornbeck testified on behalf of the commission at the opening hearing of the House Education and Labor Committee in February 1993. Hornbeck outlined the reasons why changes in Chapter 1 were important to poor children and described the commission's proposed framework. Commissioner Phyllis McClure, who also chaired the Independent Review Panel, reinforced key ideas.

In succeeding months, congressional staff members affiliated with members of the Education and Labor Committee participated in organized briefings and requested information and analysis from the commission. The media also raised questions, and the questions came from both reporters covering the reauthorization process and editorial writers. Not surprisingly, interest was strongest in formula issues, especially those involving the concentration of dollars in high-poverty schools and districts. The *Washington Post* did several editorials on the need for greater concentration. Other major dailies, including the *New York Times,* the *Philadelphia Inquirer,* and the *Los Angeles Times,* also weighed in on this issue. Most drew heavily on findings from a special research project conducted jointly by the commission and the Leadership Conference for Civil Rights that identified large numbers of high-poverty schools (defined as more than 50% poverty) in urban districts that did not receive Chapter 1 dollars, while low-poverty (less than 5% poverty) schools in nearby affluent suburbs did receive Chapter 1 dollars.

The Title I that emerged from the Education and Labor Committee, and eventually from the full House, contained many of the provisions recommended by both the commission and the Administration. If our measuring stick is fidelity to the commission's recommendations, the House proposal came closer than the Administration proposal in some regards and was further away in others. On one hand, the House proposal restricted schoolwide use of dollars to even fewer schools (setting the threshold at 60% poverty) than did the Administration and did not go nearly as far in concentrating dollars in high-poverty areas. On the other hand, the House proposal included required disaggregation of achievement data and language regarding the need for states to attend to "opportunity to learn." Neither version designated dollars specifically for professional development, a grave worry for the commission's steering committee.

Senate Deliberations

Work in the Senate got under way in March 1994. At the opening hearings, David Hornbeck once again testified about the commission's recommendations and commissioner Kati Haycock testified about the special need for whole-school improvement strategies. Commissioner Phyllis McClure also testified, again on behalf of the Independent Review Panel.

From the beginning, it was clear that the Senate bill would look much like both the Administration and the House proposals. By now, the idea of standards-based reform in Chapter 1 had been pretty much accepted. However, we believed it possible that the Senate might go further than the House in several vital areas, including schoolwide use of Chapter 1 dollars, concentration of funds in high-poverty schools, and guaranteed funding for teacher professional development.

There were, in fact, some problems in the Senate version of Title I, including an especially worrisome limitation of the high standards requirement to subjects in which Title I services are provided and a confusing prohibition on "unfunded mandates." But the Senate bill also made some major improvements, including:

- A lowering of the threshold for schoolwide use of dollars to schools with 30% poverty;
- A required set-aside of 10% of each school's dollars for professional development; and
- A provision requiring states to help school districts develop the capacity to get their students to high standards.

The conference committee worked for more than a week to resolve differences between the House and Senate bills. Most of that time was spent on Title I. For the most part, the discussions were strictly nonpartisan. The differences really were between houses, rather than parties. So-called social issues ate up much of the time. These included proposed bans on federal funding for schools that fail to expel for at least one year students who bring guns to school, that "promote homosexuality," or that interfere with "constitutionally protected" prayer. Debate on all of these issues was intense. Most were resolved with a compromise of one sort or another. Here, the votes were somewhat more partisan, but not entirely so. For example, the leadership on the gun issue came from George Miller, a liberal Democrat, and several conservative Republicans. The opposition included Bill Goodling, a moderate-to-conservative Republican, and Xavier Becerra, a liberal Democrat.

Among the most important education issues addressed by the conference committee were state responsibility for "opportunity to learn," school planning requirements, standards required in which subjects, and use of funds for professional development. The conference committee also spent considerable time devising a final formula. Indeed, the committee worked on the formula throughout the week-long conference committee session, through the weekend, and into the next week. Once again, the differences were primarily between houses, rather than parties.

That was not true when the measure went back to the House and Senate floors for final approval. By that time, *everything* that came to the floor was dealt with in a highly partisan way. And for a long while it appeared that this legislation, which had garnered strong bipartisan support all along, would go down in flames. Perhaps because of intense grassroots pressure orchestrated by the major national education organizations (which, interestingly, had seldom weighed in on the major policy issues in the bill), this final hurdle also was overcome.

The Improving America's Schools Act was signed into law by President Clinton on October 20 at a high school in Framingham, Massachusetts.

Key Changes in the New Title I Law

The new law includes many critically important program changes. Indeed, in coming years, Title I should look very different from the past.

For most of the millions of children who participated in Chapter 1, the program consisted largely of low-level remedial services, most of them provided by a Chapter 1 teacher or aide to children "pulled out" of their regular classrooms for extra help. The new law aims to replace this procedure with challenging, high-quality instruction focused on enabling poor children to reach the same high standards as other children. To accomplish this, the law seeks to change both the state policy context in which Title I schools do business and actual practices within high-poverty schools.

First, the context. Henceforth, states that wish to continue to receive Title I dollars will have new responsibilities to do the following:

- Develop high standards that specify what all children should know and be able to do.
- Develop and administer assessments at select grade levels every year to measure where children in individual schools and districts are performing in relation to those standards.
- Describe how they will ensure adequate professional development, as well as assistance for schools that wish to avail themselves of the "schoolwide" option.

- Report annually on the progress of each school and district, including information on the progress of various student groups.
- Provide assistance to schools that are not making adequate progress and ensure change in those that continue to fail.

Second, there are a number of required changes in schools and districts. New school and district responsibilities under Title I include the following:

- Districts must distribute funds in rank order of poverty regardless of grade level (which means that many districts will be funding high schools for the first time).
- Districts must develop comprehensive professional development plans.
- More schools can use the schoolwide option (the new threshold will be 50% poverty); schools that exercise this option must develop plans that focus on high-quality instruction and that otherwise describe how they will get their students to the state's standards.
- Professional development is a cornerstone of Title I. All schools must devote "sufficient" Title I resources to carry out a high-quality professional development program, and schools in need of improvement must devote a specified percentage of their funds to professional development.
- All schools — including "targeted assistance schools" — are discouraged from using remedial pull-out approaches and encouraged, instead, to work toward challenging instruction in the regular classroom and toward extended time for teaching and learning.

In short, the law envisions major changes in the way states, districts, and schools that receive Title I dollars do business. Virtually everyone — from the chief state school officer to the local superintendent to the principal, teacher, and aide in the school — is expected to do things quite differently than before.

Next Steps

Though vitally important, this law is but the first step on a much longer and much tougher journey. That journey involves the actual transformation of teaching and learning in the more than 30,000 Title I schools.

We believe that the new law provides a useful *tool* in the effort to reshape teaching and learning in schools serving poor children. It would have been a *better* tool if states had been pressed harder to attend to the enormous differences in resources and overall quality between low- and high-wealth areas. It also would have been a better tool had funding been earmarked for the high-quality professional development that all of us know will be absolutely essential to changing classroom practice. But the new law is nonetheless a useful tool.

We must all work hard to put this tool to good use. That means providing clear information about changes in the law and providing settings for local educators, parents, and others to think through how best to make a standards-based reform strategy work at the community level. That also means making tough choices when we need to — such as choosing between more aides or more professional development — and making sure that each school community has help as it seeks to transform teaching and learning. It means that central authorities must stay focused on results, rather than meddling in the means of getting there; but they also must respond forcefully when results are not forthcoming. Above all, it means that all of us must act on what research has proven time and time again, that we get from schools and students about what we expect of them. Thus we must make the leap from low standards and expectations to high standards and expectations for *all* of our students and *all* of our schools.

Members of the Commission on Chapter 1

David Hornbeck, Chair
Cynthia Brown, Director, Resource Center on Educational Equity, Council of Chief State School Officers
Edgar Cahn, Law Professor, District of Columbia Law School
Ben Canada, Superintendent, Atlanta Public Schools
Phillip Daro, New Standards Project
Kati Haycock, Director, Education Trust/AAHE
David Hornbeck, Superintendent, School District of Philadelphia
William H. Kolberg, President, National Alliance of Business
Henry Levin, Director, Center for Educational Research, Stanford University
George Madaus, Director, Center for the Study of Testing, Boston College
Phyllis McClure, Education Consultant
Hayes Mizell, Director, Program for Disadvantaged Youth, The Edna McConnell Clark Foundation
Joe Nathan, Director, Center for School Reform, Humphrey Institute, University of Minnesota

Susana Navarro, Director, Southwest Center for Academic Excellence, University of Texas at El Paso
Bertha Pendleton, Superintendent of Schools, San Diego Unified School District
Diane Piche, Attorney
Delia Pompa, National Coalition of Advocates for Students
Al Ramirez, Director of Education, Iowa Department of Education
Sharon Robinson, Assistant Secretary, U.S. Department of Education
Bella Rosenberg, Assistant to the President, American Federation of Teachers
Ramsey Selden, Director, State Education Assessment Center, Council of Chief State School Officers
Robert Slavin, Director, Elementary School Programs
James Smith, Senior Vice President, National Board of Professional Teaching Standards
Marshall Smith, Under Secretary, Department of Education
William Taylor, Attorney
Marc Tucker, President, National Center for Education and the Economy
Brenda Turnbull, Principal, Policy Studies Associates
Rafael Valdivieso, Vice President, Academy for Educational Development
Paul Weckstein, Director, Center for Law and Education
Anne Wheelock, Center for Improvement of Urban Education
Robert Witherspoon, Education Consultant

PART III
OTHER MAJOR PROGRAMS

Professional Development and Education Reform

By Congressman Thomas C. Sawyer

Democrat Thomas C. Sawyer is in his fifth term representing the 14th Congressional District of Ohio. He was first elected to the U.S. House of Representatives in 1986.

Previously, Mr. Sawyer served as mayor of Akron, Ohio. Elected in 1983, he was the first Democrat to win election as Akron's mayor in 20 years. Prior to that service as mayor, he ran successfully for the Ohio House of Representatives in 1976. In all instances, he has been deeply involved in education issues.

Mr. Sawyer received his bachelor's and master's degrees from the University of Akron. He taught in the Cleveland, Ohio, public school system and worked as an administrator at a state school for delinquent boys before entering politics.

From teeming urban centers to remote areas of hardscrabble rural poverty and everywhere in between, federal programs bringing aid to American education have grown and evolved over the last 30 years. Broad-based and highly focused categorical assistance has flowed from Washington to every school system in the United States through the Elementary and Secondary Education Act, reauthorized every five years by the U.S. Congress.

Some of its elements have worked better than others, and we often take them for granted. Others have been less successful, or circumstances have changed; and those efforts have changed over time. Still others have simply failed in their missions; some of those have died, some remain in need of better focus.

Thorough review of all these elements has characterized recent education reform on the federal level, and teacher training and professional development are powerful tools in making old and new elements work together.

It was clear from the beginning that the 1994 reauthorization of ESEA, called the Improving America's Schools Act, would depart from the incremental changes that had characterized ESEA's first three decades. It had to do so for many reasons. Dollars are scarce. The nation is more diverse and changing more rapidly than at any time in this century. What may have worked a decade ago may not work today. The stakes in terms of the nation's future are higher than at any time in living memory. And the eyes of every citizen are on America's schools.

The 1994 act adopted several approaches to accomplishing real, strategic change in the federal role in aid to education. These approaches included eliminating and consolidating some programs; strengthening others; driving program dollars directly to local schools where they can do the most good; minimizing, where possible, administrative interference and cost at the state and federal levels; encouraging flexibility in the use of federal dollars in combination with state, local, and private-sector funding; and rewarding schools that work together with other schools, colleges and universities, libraries and museums, places of employment, and other institutions and agencies.

All these things are important, to be sure. However, almost from the moment the ink was dry on the agreement between President Bush and the state governors at the 1989 Education Summit in Charlottesville, one thing above all was clear: The quality of the nation's teaching force would be a central and critical feature of education reform.

Let me step back for a moment.

It was spring 1957. Miss Barber, my sixth-grade science teacher, was reviewing the items on our end-of-the-year test. One of the questions asked was:

> Men in space would have to wear space suits due to:
>
> (a) atomic radiation in space.
> (b) extreme heat in space.
> (c) extreme cold in space.
> (d) all of the above.
> (e) none of the above.

I had circled (e), and it had a big X through it. It seemed to me that none of the choices was even close to reflecting the need to compensate for the absence of atmospheric pressure in space. So I raised my hand when we got to that question and asked Miss Barber what the right answer was.

She was very kind and patient. She said that many of us had missed this one and asked me to turn to a certain page and read aloud to the class:

If men ever go into space, they will have to wear specially designed space suits. Without such protection in space, their blood would actually boil.

"So you see," she said, "the correct answer is (b)." She explained that this was a test of our deductive reasoning, and she offered us a short lesson in the importance of careful reasoning in science.

Miss Barber was a good teacher, but she was not prepared to teach a curriculum that she had never studied and that must have seemed to be changing as rapidly as the daily newspaper.

The truth is that it was.

Times of great change are always difficult for societies to manage. Change affects all of us, but in America it has influenced education in particularly important ways.

We Have Been There Before

At the end of the last century, the United States emerged as a modern industrial power; and with it came the growth of education as an instrument of nation building. That growth took many forms: the Morrill Acts for the building of practical Land Grant colleges and the widespread emergence of normal schools for the training of teachers, the spread of larger city school systems from the East throughout the newly industrialized Midwest, the gradual demise of the one-room schoolhouse and the one-building school system, the development of vocational training as an important function in building the productive capacity of the nation and its communities, the accommodation in schools of the needs of the largest waves of immigration in the nation's history, and the rise of the states in the exercise of their responsibility over all these complex changes and more.

If all this sounds familiar, it should. The era is remarkably similar to our own. But change of this kind was a profound shock to Miss Barber and to the nation nearly 40 years ago.

The response began with the now familiar passage of the National Defense Education Act and was followed by enactment of laws bringing federal aid to education throughout the United States. From a specialized program to bring science and pre-engineering education to the best and brightest of the nation's students, there grew an effort to equalize access to learning for even the most educationally disadvantaged kids across this large, diverse country.

Many forces from every level and location throughout the country drove the nation's policy makers together in Charlottesville five years ago. However, the consensus was that the achievement levels of American students lagged behind those of their international peers. That shared concern resulted in the formulation of the now well-known six education goals and the enactment of the Goals 2000: Educate America Act.

That legislation became a framework for action, a vehicle for the nation's government to bring assistance to states and local schools as they crafted their own brands of education reform. It recognized that no two places are exactly alike, and so reform must be geared to the different areas of the country and the states and individual communities.

It also recognized that, over time, problems had grown throughout the nation that were more or less common to communities of every size and description. Foremost among these, and central to them, was an understanding that teaching and learning still was based on knowledge and skills best suited to the needs *of another era.*

The curriculum that teachers are being asked to teach, and students to learn, all across the nation was derived from that time a century ago when we moved into the modern industrial period. The changes in content and teaching technique; in textbooks, materials, and classroom facilities; and in so many other practical aspects of teaching and learning have been so gradual that they would have been familiar stuff to teachers of Miss Barber's generation and those from whom she learned a generation earlier. The Xerox machine, after all, is not so different from the mimeograph, except that the teacher's fingers aren't as likely to be stained purple. And the computer hardware, available to most kids for only a limited period, is only marginally more effective than the old filmstrip.

The fact is that for most classrooms, the chalkboard and the textbook still go hand in hand with paper and pencil as the primary tools of teaching and learning. The American classroom is isolated in technique, in curricular content, and in the tools of instruction. The world has changed; but in so many ways, the school has not.

But this is not to say that work is not already well under way in each of these arenas.

The Beginning of Modern Reform

For more than a decade, the National Council of Teachers of Mathematics (NCTM) has been working to develop and publish high-quality, internationally competitive content standards for math courses from the earliest elementary years through high school. They have analyzed what we expect kids to know and to be able to do in the logic, language, and technique of math, and they have built a model curriculum around it. They are developing the textual materials, student workbooks, instructional equipment, and software — in short, everything needed to present a comprehensive, sophisticated subject with its full range of knowledge and skills that students are expected to master.

Further, the council is writing and testing the student performance standards needed to align with that curriculum and the instructional materials to go with them. To ensure real achievement of those performance standards and to measure student progress in real time and in real classroom settings, NCTM is developing new assessments — tests — that are more than hurdles in a student's path. They are designed to provide continuous diagnosis of a child's progress, allowing teachers to accelerate or slow instruction as needed to ensure full attainment before moving ahead with new material. Finally, NCTM is working to ensure that teachers themselves are fully prepared to teach these skills, as well as having mastered the material themselves, through model undergraduate training and professional licensure.

Three years after the publication of the NCTM standards, their approach was given additional momentum with the passage of the Goals 2000: Educate America Act.

Unlike reform efforts of the past, the strategy of systemic reform seeks to fit together the different parts of the system in a much more unified way. What we expect students to learn has to be in the textbooks they use; the textbooks must be closely aligned with overall curriculum goals; tests need to reflect what we expect students to know; and teachers must be able to understand and teach that content. In a very real sense, teacher training is the connective tissue among all of these elements. A much greater investment in the preparation and continuous training of the teaching force will be the critical link in the systemic reform chain. The real promise for improved student achievement that the standards represent will not be realized unless teachers can master the subject matter and pedagogical skills that undergird them. In fact, Congress considered the professional development of teachers of such importance that it amended the original list of education goals to include a new Goal 4:

> By the year 2000, the Nation's teaching force will have access to programs for the continued improvement of their professional skills and the opportunity to acquire the knowledge and skills needed to instruct and prepare all American students for the next century.

Can the Existing Teacher Training System be Retooled?

Yes, it probably can. But we *must* acknowledge why the current system is inadequate and where the real problems lie.

First, the sheer size of the teaching force will make change difficult. As of 1994, 2,550,000 men and women were teaching in public elementary and secondary schools, and 370,000 were teaching in private schools. Ensuring that content-based reform reaches that many people will be difficult and potentially expensive. Moreover, a large cohort of the current teacher workforce is nearing retirement age in the last half of this decade. Not only will they be difficult to replace all at once, but they will not be available even informally to mentor their successors.

Second, the very nature of teaching could impede reform. Teachers teach alone, isolated from each other and from administrators. Only a tiny number teach in teams, and even fewer participate in regular professional development networks that promote serious communication about teaching practices or changing curriculum.

Third, very little of the governance structure of most public schools is in the hands of teachers. Teachers are not given the support and responsibilities enjoyed by professionals in other careers. They have little control over their daily schedules and frequently do not participate in decisions that affect their classroom teaching.

Fourth, and perhaps most important, current teacher education programs often are poorly suited to the real instructional needs of classroom teachers. Many current preservice teacher training programs lack the challenge and rigor to attract the best undergraduates to the teaching profession. Too often, they consist of dog-and-pony workshops, motivational speeches packaged like minstrel shows, or shills peddling software, hardware, workbooks, and other set-piece curriculum items like the patent medicines of old. Anecdotal evidence strongly suggests that new graduates are not well-prepared to face the challenging realities of their initial classroom assignments. Inservice teacher training opportunities are too brief and episodic and are not focused on updated content or state-of-the-art pedagogy.

A Workable Model for Expanded Professional Development

Designing a tightly focused professional development program became an important priority in the reauthorization of ESEA. In a very real sense, the success of everything else we wanted to achieve depended on it. Fortunately, the Education Committee did not have to start from scratch to design an entirely new program. We already had a working model for professional development, the Dwight D. Eisenhower Math and Science Education Act or, as it is fondly known, IKE. It contains several critically important features that *should* form the core of any larger professional development plan. And it works.

Most important, teacher training activities under IKE are locally designed and flexible in order to allow individual communities to make adaptations that meet their own needs. Many local school districts have formed creative and collaborative relationships with one another and with institutions of higher education in their regions to build lasting and substantive programs of professional development. IKE encouraged and rewarded the formation of consortia so that schools and school districts with common needs could work together. It was one of the of the earliest education enactments that assisted with funding the formation of such partnerships. It built on the demonstrated success that education institutions, businesses, and the foundation and nonprofit communities had long enjoyed.

For 10 years, the Six-District Educational Compact Mathematics and Science Project in my own congressional district has built a partnership among six school systems, the State Department of Education, several universities, and such major industries as IBM and the Goodyear Tire and Rubber Company. In the compact, the Eisenhower federal funding is at the core of the partnership. This "earnest money" is a magnet that is both an organizing tool and a way to bring others who are committed to the same goals into the compact. Resource teams, which span grades K-12, include teachers, principals, subject matter experts, and representatives of participating colleges and universities. The central mission of the compact is to provide lasting professional growth through rigorous and credible staff development and, in so doing, to improve the achievement levels of students.

The model used by the compact has proven very successful and continues to attract new participants and the support of the wider community. It involves many teachers and helps create leaders and teaching teams in schools, while avoiding a "top-down" approach. If systemic reform is really going to work, this is how it will actually happen.

The Eisenhower programs vary widely across the nation precisely because of their broad-based, bottom-up approach. One-third of all U.S. teachers have some exposure to Eisenhower-supported activities at some time during the academic year, and we have learned as much from the handful of flawed programs as we have from its growing number of successes.

The chief criticism of the Eisenhower math and science program has been that it supported inservice training opportunities that were not of sufficient duration and intensity. But that is true of what passes for professional development or teacher inservice training in too many places, regardless of IKE. Because federal resources have been limited, dollars sometimes are spread too thinly, limiting quality. But as funds have increased, and where local districts have well-developed plans that include consortia and public-private partnerships, some noteworthy progress has been made.

IKE is well suited to form the core of a larger professional development program. First, it is a program focused on the professional development needs of teachers in two important core academic subjects: math and science. The achievement levels of American students are dangerously low in these areas, and widely accepted math curriculum standards are already in use. Science standards are close to completion.

Second, this program succeeds because there is a strong sense of ownership by classroom teachers, and its programs are designed and administered very close to actual teachers in actual classrooms. The new Eisenhower Professional Development Program, which is now Part II of ESEA, will expand the focus of the Eisenhower program beyond math and science to include all the core academic subjects, in effect linking professional development to achieving the National Education Goals.

Professional development that is aligned with the new content standards and governed by a decision making that is controlled by local teachers is a powerful engine for the improvement of the training of our professional teaching force.

The new law contains important new provisions. For instance, one new provision will require both the state and local education agencies applying for federal funding to have in place a plan outlining how they will meet the professional development needs of all teachers and how those plans are consistent with state content and performance standards. Right now, many classroom teachers voice a common complaint that the limited professional development opportunities that they do have are selected by others and have little relevance to their particular classroom challenges. This is an essential point. The new law provides the opportunity for teachers to significantly influence both the choice and the design of professional development activities. Local professional development plans must be developed by classroom teachers from all the core subjects and from each of the appropriate grade spans.

Real success will depend on teamwork at the local level and the ability to adapt the program to local needs.

In that sense, the chief strength of the new Eisenhower professional development program is its elasticity. Under the new program, school districts will be required to maintain funding for their current math and science programs; but beyond that, there are few restrictions. This maintenance of effort in math and science is intended to protect progress in these two critical areas. However, it also recognizes that the planning process for each subject depends on the content standards themselves. So although we already have widely accepted math standards and are very close to having science standards, local school districts still will have time to plan for new standards in English, geography, history, and other subjects.

Under the new law, local school districts, with the active participation of teachers, must conduct a needs analysis to help them evaluate their professional development program design. There will be choices to make. If local school districts maintain their previous investments in training for math and science teachers, their decisions will be influenced only by the results of their needs analysis and the availability of standards-based curriculum.

Role of the States

State-level activities and technical assistance will be important elements in local efforts to build and reinforce professional development capacity. These state-level activities should include: 1) reforming state licensure for teachers and other educators to ensure that it is aligned with curriculum content standards, 2) developing performance assessments and peer-review procedures for licensure, 3) assisting in the creation of high-quality professional development and curricula in districts and schools, 4) supporting professional development networks on a state and regional basis, 5) facilitating the formation of partnerships between schools or districts and higher education institutions, and 6) strengthening the capacity of teachers to integrate education technologies into their instruction.

In a very real sense, the central mission of this new professional development program will be to move teachers and their students together, toward the same goals, developing a set of highly adaptable and transferable skills that are as meaningful in Montana as they are in New York or Ohio.

Can We Finance a National Professional Development Program?

Surely the answer to that question is no — if we see the federal treasury as a sole funding option. But the new Eisenhower Professional Development Program recognizes that this is not only unlikely but undesirable. The financial burdens faced by just about every school district in this country are monumental. School superintendents everywhere say the same thing: Training opportunities for classroom teachers are one of the first things to be cut when a fiscal crisis looms. This is a terrible choice that school administrators should never have to make.

Professional development needs to be a priority in every school in every district. The new Eisenhower Professional Development Program will help. It requires each local school district that applies for these funds to provide a 33% local match for the total number of federal dollars. This is not a strict dollar-for-dollar match, however. The law is intentionally flexible. This match can be met in a variety of ways, such as calculating the cost of release time for teachers participating in training programs. The use of state funds and funds from other federal programs, such as Title I, Bilingual Education, Goals 2000, and others, also can be used to meet the match, as can local dollars, contributions — direct and in-kind — from private sources.

This match is not to serve as an accounting or auditing bludgeon. It is really a device to compel a serious and creative commitment on the part of schools and districts. It also will help school districts to systematically coordinate the expenditure of funds from a variety of sources and to focus them on the professional development needs of their teachers. It should work. If it does not, the state may waive the matching for schools or districts that can demonstrate extraordinary financial hardship.

Hoping to strengthen teacher training even further, the Administration initially proposed combining the Chapter 2 program and the Eisenhower program into a new $800 million professional development program. With the local 33% match, it would have created a professional development program with more than $1 billion dedicated to the goal of helping educators develop their craft. However, the Chapter 2 program is popular because of its flexibility. It is a program of broad purposes that assists state and local education agencies in improving quality and promoting innovation in elementary and secondary schools. In 1994, for instance, it provided about $379 million for a range of activities in six areas, including professional development, school reform, and the purchase of educational technology and library materials. School districts are free to choose their own areas of focus and priority.

Who would not like that? Where Chapter 2 funding is used carefully, the effect is positive. The issue of Chapter 2's popularity was never in doubt. The only question was whether, in this era of strictly limited funding, it was the best use of scarce federal dollars. From time to time, we re-examine the effectiveness of the federal role in American education. There are many good reasons for doing this. The money the federal government spends on education represents a small fraction of combined federal, state, and local expenditures. But the money spent by the federal government is different. It is designed to achieve purposes of national significance and to encourage activities that would not occur in its absence. In other words, if the purpose of federal funding to education is to engender effective change, it is important to be able to evaluate it. The Chapter 2 program simply does not meet that test. Its funding often is used only to supplement long-established state and local expenditure patterns.

But, in the end, the lure of Chapter 2's flexibility won the day. Unfortunately, this means that both the new Eisenhower Professional Development Program and Chapter 2 will remain on the books, locked in a head-to-head competition for limited funding.

Conclusion

If we as a nation, or as individual communities, were going to outline how we might plan a new education system, we could not do better than to model our efforts on the innovative and collaborative professional development activities under way throughout the country today.

The problem, perhaps the core problem for education reformers at the end of the 20th century, is that ours is an already mature system. Its roots lie in the birth of the nation, and its fundamentals have not undergone real change for most of the century. The people we depend on to carry out that change are many, vary widely in their own levels of skill mastery, and are isolated from one another for all practical purposes.

These problems also are not unique to education. But in almost every arena of modern enterprise, we have come to accept that *learning* needs to become as much a part of daily life in the workplace as *work* itself. And yet, we expect that teachers, once they receive their credentials, are prepared to span a 30-year career using the same skills with which they began. It did not work for Miss Barber in a far more static era. And it surely will not work for her grandchildren in teaching today. In a time of enormous change, no other thought-intensive endeavor in our society relies on such a fragile notion.

The Chapter 2 Program

By Congressman Steve Gunderson

Republican Steve Gunderson is in his eighth term representing the 3rd Congressional District of Wisconsin. He was first elected to the U.S. House of Representatives in 1980. He currently serves on the House Economic and Educational Opportunities Committee and the House Agriculture Committee.

Previously, Mr. Gunderson served three terms in the Wisconsin State Assembly. He received his bachelor's degree from the University of Wisconsin-Madison in 1974.

Over the last four decades, educators, parents, and legislators have struggled in defining the roles that the federal, state, and local governments play in education. The debate intensified in the 103rd Congress, which will go down in history as the most successful "Education Congress."

The education agenda of the 103rd Congress included the passage of the following legislative initiatives: Goals 2000, School-to-Work Opportunities Act, National and Community Service Trust Act, and the Elementary and Secondary Education Act. Goals 2000 and the Elementary and Secondary Education Act are the two primary examples where considerable debate occurred regarding the appropriate functions of the federal, state, and local governments in our education system.

The education proposals passed in 1993 and 1994 had one common theme — reform. In both Goals 2000 and the restructured Chapter 2 Program, Congress responded to the calls from state and local education agencies that they be given the flexibility, within certain parameters, to respond to the education reform needs in their communities.

The focus of this section is the 1994 reauthorization of the Chapter 2 Program. In order to better understand the debate that transpired on this reauthorization effort, it may be helpful to briefly review the history of the program.

The Chapter 2 Program originated under the Omnibus Budget Reconciliation Act of 1981. The idea, conceived by the Reagan Administration, was the result of consolidating 38 categorical programs into a new education block grant. The purpose of this new block grant was to give local education agencies the flexibility to respond to the specific education needs of individual communities. A local school district could use all of the dollars for a single education program or for an array of activities.

Chapter 2's flexibility is its greatest attribute. School districts throughout the United States have benefited from Chapter 2 funds by using the dollars for school improvement planning, expanding curriculum development, promoting education through technology, and systemic reform. On 25 May 1993, Dr. Joan Ruskus, a senior researcher at SRI International, presented research at a House Education and Labor Committee hearing that showed that three-fourths of all school districts in her study used Chapter 2 funding to support local school district priorities.

In the original Chapter 2 authorization, several guidelines were listed to assist local education agencies in structuring their initiatives. These included: programs for at-risk students, acquisition of educational materials, schoolwide improvement efforts, professional development, and other innovative projects aimed at improving a school's environment. My home state of Wisconsin has closely followed the original guidelines. Wisconsin's school districts have used their Chapter 2 allocation predominantly for the purchase of computers and teaching computer classes. In addition, Wisconsin has concentrated much of its Chapter 2 effort on programs for at-risk children by promoting literacy initiatives for children and their parents.

As the Congress began its 1993-1994 deliberations on the Elementary and Secondary Education Act, it was clear that the merits of the Chapter 2 program would be discussed thoroughly. Several elements led to the fiery debate.

First, the Department of Education released a 1994 report, *How Chapter 2 Operates at the Federal, State, and Local Levels,* that laid the foundation for the latest reauthorization. The report stated emphatically that local Chapter 2 dollars should focus on education reform initiatives.

Second, President Clinton's "Improving America's Schools Act" (his version of the Elementary and Secondary Reauthorization Act) called for the merger of Chapter 2 with a professional development program. This merger would allocate most of these dollars for teacher training activities.

Third, the sentiment of some members of Congress and of some education experts was that the Chapter 2 Program was too diverse. It was believed that, in some instances, dollars were being expended on projects that were not necessarily priorities for local school districts.

These three points were examined carefully to determine how to make the Chapter 2 Program more responsive to the needs of 21st century students. The arguments regarding Chapter 2's future were very contentious. Some in Congress felt very strongly that by creating a separate Professional Development Section, another section for technology, and a section devoted to school library media projects, the Chapter 2 Program was obsolete.

I and Congressmen Bill Goodling (R-Pennsylvania), at the time the ranking Republican member of the House Education and Labor Committee and now the Chairman of that committee, adamantly refuted this logic. We argued that the Chapter 2 Program must be continued because local school districts should have the ability to design their own initiatives to meet their own individual needs. School districts should not be limited to carrying out projects only related to computers, professional development, and library media efforts — all meritorious programs.

The Chapter 2 discussion is perhaps one of the best illustrations of the constant struggle over the roles of the federal, state, and local governments. Those who opposed the reauthorization of Chapter 2 contended that state and local education agencies should not be given federal dollars to use at their own discretion. The Chapter 2 advocates believed that state and local education agencies generally have a better understanding of how to make the best use of federal funds if certain parameters are created.

Rewriting Chapter 2 required maintaining a balance between flexibility and making the program more focused. The compromise legislation accomplished this difficult goal. Chapter 2, as enacted in 1994, contains the following significant changes:

1. Moving Chapter 2 to its own title within the 1994 Elementary and Secondary Education Act. Chapter 2 is now Title VI of the Elementary and Secondary Education Act and is called Innovative Education Program Strategies.
2. The purpose has been revamped drastically to emphasize that projects funded under the new Title VI be aligned closely with reform strategies.
3. Program strategies should be devised that will work toward accomplishing the National Education Goals.

4. The allocation of dollars to local education agencies increased from 80% to 85%.

The Chapter 2 reauthorization debate is one that will continue and intensify over the next several years. All of us will continue the struggle to find the appropriate mechanisms so that every elementary and secondary student will receive the essential skills for participation in a high tech, global workforce.

As we continue to search for the right formula or formulas for education improvement, we need to decide the roles the federal, state, and local governments should play in carrying out that mission. It is fitting that the Chapter 2 Program was scrutinized in the 103rd Congress, the Congress that marked the end of 40 years of Democratic control. For it is the Chapter 2 Program, one of the first Reagan education block grant programs to be enacted, that may set the stage for the various education proposals that will come before the Republican-controlled Congress.

Beyond Ideology: Educating Language-Minority Children Through the ESEA

By Congressman Xavier Becerra

Democrat Xavier Becerra was elected in 1992 to represent California's 30th Congressional District, located in Los Angeles. He serves on three standing committees in the House of Representatives, including Economic and Educational Opportunities; was the Freshman Democratic Caucus Whip; and is a member of the Congressional Hispanic Caucus.

Mr. Becerra is a former California Deputy Attorney General and began his legal career in 1984 in a legal services office representing the mentally ill. He received a bachelor's degree in economics from Stanford University in 1980 and a J.D. in 1984 from Stanford Law School.

According to the 1990 Census, 13.9% of all children aged 5 to 17 in the United States spoke a language other than English at home. That represents a 41.2% increase between 1980 and 1990 in the population of school-age children who usually speak a language other than English during a period that also had a 4% decline in school enrollment. This dramatic growth of the school-age language-minority population — children whose native language is not English — is the result of a combination of several factors, including history, demography, and immigration.

Contrary to popular opinion, most language-minority students are native-born Americans. Many of their parents attended U.S. schools and are, themselves, the victims of prior discrimination and educational neglect. Because many language-minority communities include a high percentage of younger residents, there is certain to be continued growth in language-minority student enrollments even before immigration comes into play.

During the last decade, more than two million immigrant youth enrolled in public schools nationwide. Limited-English-proficient (LEP) students — those who lack English skills and are at grave risk of educational failure when enrolled in academic programs conducted only in English — make up a significant part of that population.

This latest wave of immigration differs significantly from the last wave, which occurred at the beginning of this century. The immigration wave of 1910-1920 was predominantly European; this wave comes from diverse cultures, speaking literally hundreds of different languages. For example, in 1989 New York reported that immigrant students who had been in the United States for three years or less came from 162 different countries. In 1990, California reported that LEP students in the state spoke 46 different primary languages.[1] This diversity poses both great possibilities and challenges for our schools.

With an increasingly global economy, our children can benefit from exposure to different cultures and languages. The linguistic skills and cultural knowledge that language-minority students bring to school are invaluable resources that deserve to be developed and shared for the benefit of all students. However, our schools must be prepared to take advantage of this opportunity. If they are not, our children will not be prepared to work, learn, interact, and lead globally. The Elementary and Secondary Education Act (ESEA) is the embodiment of the possibility and the challenge facing our schools. The programs it sponsors have the potential to make our classrooms truly global.

The Bilingual Education Act

The year we began consideration of the Elementary and Secondary Education Act reauthorization, 1993, marked the 25th anniversary of Title VII, the Bilingual Education Act. This was the first federal education program focused on the needs of language-minority students.

Although Title VII has been chronically underfunded — especially during the 1980s, when the real (inflation-adjusted) level of appropriations fell by nearly 50% — it has served to lead state and local education agencies in the development of special programs for LEP students. The program has leveraged positive educational change responsive to the growing linguistic and cultural diversity in American schools. Specifically, Title VII has:

- provided grants to local education agencies for the development

and implementation of new programs specifically designed for non-English-speaking students;
- provided grants to institutions of higher education, which made possible the preservice and inservice training of tens of thousands of education personnel who work with language-minority and LEP populations; and
- supported specialized training and technical assistance centers and a national clearinghouse on bilingual education, as well as centers to assist state and local education agencies in the development of reliable program assessment methods.

Demographic trends underscore the importance of not just maintaining but strengthening and expanding the federal Bilingual Education Act. The federal government has played a major role in helping schools develop the capacity to deliver effective instruction to students with special needs. However, despite the substantial progress generated by Title VII, the need for national leadership and federal assistance will continue for the foreseeable future.

Chapter 1

Changes in ESEA's Chapter 1, the largest federal elementary and secondary education program, also were needed. As a result of this reauthorization, Chapter 1 has been transformed from a "compensatory," "remedial" education program for poor children into a program that enables poor students to achieve the highest standards. Chapter 1 also was revised to address the educational needs and strengths of LEP students.

A recent study demonstrates that Chapter 1 has not been serving LEP students equitably or effectively. According to the study, local school systems understood that the purpose of Chapter 1 was to overcome poor children's educational disadvantage by providing them with supplemental remedial services. However, it was mistakenly believed that bilingual or ESL instruction was a substitute for Chapter 1 and that Chapter 1 services should be delivered only in English. Schools were further confused by a rule requiring schools to differentiate between educational disadvantage and limited-English-proficiency in determining whether a student was eligible for services under Chapter 1. This served to exclude LEP students rather than to encourage their participation. Thus the relatively few LEP students receiving Chapter 1 services were served in an ineffective manner, as a result of a system ill-prepared for a diverse student population.[2]

It was in this context that the Hispanic Caucus considered the impending reauthorization and chose to make this issue a priority.

Efforts of the Congressional Hispanic Caucus

In response to the need for major changes in both Chapter 1 and Title VII, the Congressional Hispanic Caucus introduced legislation, H.R. 3229, which addressed the most pressing issues for reform within the ESEA.

With little difficulty and with bipartisan support, Title VII of H.R. 6, the omnibus committee bill to reauthorize ESEA, incorporated most of the provisions of the Hispanic Caucus bill. Under H.R. 6, Title VII would continue as a discretionary, competitive, capacity-building program with the same superstructure of current law, but with significant changes. Some of the major changes include:

- an expansion of local grants to encompass schoolwide and districtwide efforts;
- an emphasis on bilingualism as an outcome of Title VII, establishing a funding priority for "applications which provide for the development of bilingual proficiency for all participating students"; and
- an emphasis on staff development, family education, and intensification of instruction by expanding the education calendar, encouraging the use of new technology, expanding the use of professional and volunteer aides, and providing supplementary programs and services at times when school is not in session.

With the same level of bipartisan cooperation, critical provisions of the Hispanic Caucus bill were included in Chapter 1 of the committee bill. The negative, self-fulfilling notion of educational disadvantage was eliminated from the program. Chapter 1 now is oriented toward helping poor children — all poor children — achieve high standards. Specifically:

- Chapter 1 no longer excludes children on the basis of their limited-English-proficiency.
- Chapter 1 programs must specifically address the needs and strengths of LEP students.
- All parents, including those who are limited in their English proficiency, must be informed about and involved in their children's education.

- Provisions were included to ensure the accuracy and fairness of Chapter 1 student and program assessments involving LEP students.

The Hispanic Caucus was proud to have played an important role in the development of H.R. 6. The bill included real solutions to difficulties faced by language-minority students across the nation. However, the legislation did not pass without challenge.

Hostile Amendments

Of course, there were those who would eliminate programs that teach bilingualism. In an early hearing, Representative Toby Roth (R-Wis.), in reference to a bill he introduced, the Declaration of Official Language Act, said, "I feel we are all Americans and there is no need for hyphenated Americans. A key part of this bill is the elimination of the failed bilingual education programs. . . . Programs such as bilingual education which actually inhibit the learning of English must be eliminated." In response, Representative Lynn Woolsey (D-Calif.) pronounced, "We don't ask these children to give up their native tongue, because that is going to be to their benefit in the long run and the closer we come as a nation to being monolingual, the less competitive we will be in the industrial world."

With an open rule permitting virtually any amendment to be filed in advance of the debate, the stage was set for a heated contest between those who would have English as the sole language spoken in America and those who considered bilingualism an asset rather than an albatross. As we had suspected, several amendments along these lines were filed. Representative Dana Rohrbacher (R-Calif.) filed two amendments with respect to student and family immigration status, and Representative Roth filed two amendments with respect to bilingual education.

On 3 March 1994, the House took up the first amendment introduced by Mr. Rohrbacher. Under that amendment, school districts would be required to report to the Department of Education annually "the total number of students enrolled in its school system, the number of students enrolled who are not lawfully in the United States, the number of students who are lawfully in the United States who do not have at least one parent or legal guardian who is lawfully in the United States, and the average per pupil expenditure of the local educational agency."

For almost three hours, members passionately debated for and against the amendment. Five members spoke in favor of the amendment, and 21 spoke against; an additional five members filed written statements in opposition to the amendment.

Mr. Rohrbacher felt that his was a "non-controversial" amendment. He explained, "To those who believe that the Federal Government should provide such compensation to school districts with high levels of illegal immigrants, this amendment will provide them the data they need to determine the amount of money that is needed to be reimbursed. Those who believe, as I do, that Government should not provide education for illegal aliens and their children will also find it valuable to have these costs and the figures available."

Education and Labor Committee Chairman William D. Ford (D-Mich.), an unabashed and outspoken champion of children, was the first to speak in opposition to the amendment, saying, "I am opposed to the Gentleman's amendment because it is insane to suggest that after what we learned about Nazi Germany in the period before World War II, that we would turn little children into informers on their parents as to their nationality status in schools in this country and expect that they would still go to school with trust in their eyes and trust in their hearts." Representative Ford continued, "Not since Adolf Hitler has any government asked little school children to tell on mommy and daddy."

Reflecting the bipartisan nature of the opposition to the amendment, Representative Ileana Ros-Lehtinen (R-Fla.) and Representative Constance Morella (R-Md.) offered two of the most stirring statements of the debate. Their comments follow.

> As a certified teacher, I am sensitive to the education ramifications of such a damaging amendment, and as someone who came to the United States at an early age and learned English through a bilingual program, I cannot stress to my colleagues enough that we cannot allow this and other harmful amendments to pass today. ... I am also worried about the implications for blameless children and families who are citizens of the United States but who do not look like an antiquated version of what an "average American" might be, and who, therefore, may be susceptible to discrimination. (Representative Ileana Ros-Lehtinen)

> The Rohrbacher Amendment is punitive, mean-spirited, and unconstitutional. Why should we punish children for the actions of their parents? Our students represent the future of our Nation. We must educate all of our children, for they are the citizens of tomorrow and our future workers. In 1982, the Supreme Court handed down a decision that all undocumented children have a right to a public education in the case *Plyler* v. *Doe*. The Rohrbacher

amendment clearly contradicts the Supreme Court decision which affirms that basic education cannot be denied to any child. Mr. Chairman, I recognize and uphold the right of the United States to protect its borders and regulate immigration. The Rohrbacher amendment would do nothing to address concerns regarding illegal immigration. Instead, it would have a detrimental effect on children, and ultimately on the future of our nation. (Representative Constance Morella)

The house rejected the amendment by 329 to 78.

The second amendment relating to immigration was intended to strike the Bilingual Education Act from the reauthorization bill. Again, the debate was fast and furious, with a lopsided margin speaking against the amendment. My office worked closely with the Congressional Hispanic Caucus and others in waging a campaign against the amendment. Our efforts included several "Dear Colleague" letters to inform the debate, as well as alerting national education organizations, school districts, and civil rights and advocacy organizations as to the seriousness of this threat. With an overwhelming defeat (334 to 58), Mr. Roth elected not to offer his second amendment, which was designed to recast Title VII as a remedial English-acquisition program.

The final critical amendment regarding bilingual education was offered by Representative Rohrbacher on March 22. That amendment would have barred any funds authorized under ESEA from being used to provide any benefit or assistance to illegal aliens. This amendment was defeated by voice vote.

The introduction of these amendments and the real threat they initially posed are not so much a comment on the state of bilingual education as they are a reflection of the mean-spirited anti-immigrant sentiment that has infected so many debates on a wide variety of proposals. In the last year, the House has considered amendments to restrict benefits to undocumented immigrants in such diverse measures as earthquake relief, extension of unemployment benefits, national service programs, and arts programs. It is unfortunate that an attribute such as bilingualism, which should be so attractive in this global economy, is so belittled.

The decisive defeat of the Rohrbacher and Roth amendments was the product of an unprecedented collaborative effort involving almost the entire education community and responsible leaders from both parties in Congress. It represents the triumph of rational, humane, bipartisan lawmaking. It is my hope that it will serve as a model for future legislation.

Passage in the House

The Elementary and Secondary Education Act was passed in the house by a vote of 289 to 128. The House legislation represented a major advance in federal education policy, especially as it relates to the education of limited-English-proficient students and their families. With respect to both Title VII, the Bilingual Education Act, and Chapter 1, the largest federal elementary and secondary education program, H.R. 6 incorporates almost all of the features of the bipartisan Congressional Hispanic Caucus bill.

H.R. 6 redesignates Chapter 1 as Title I, the name originally given to the 1965 program for economically disadvantaged students. The new Title I program is revamped to:

- stress systemic educational improvement, rather than remedial services;
- emphasize high academic standards, schoolwide programming, comprehensive child services through the coordination of resources available under different federal programs, parent involvement, authentic assessment of student progress, and ongoing staff development; and
- develop Title I programs and services that are educationally appropriate for LEP students.

Because of the enormous resources available under the Title I program, and the fact that most LEP students meet the poverty eligibility requirements, the reforms of the Title I program brought about through H.R. 6 will prove to be of great value to limited-English-proficient students and the educators who serve them.

The ESEA reauthorization also provided an opportunity to retool the Bilingual Education Act into an instrument of systemic school reform and educational excellence. As reauthorized, ESEA provides a strong foundation for a new generation of bilingual education programs. The House bill:

- Expands grants to support schoolwide and districtwide efforts to improve educational opportunities for limited-English-proficient students.
- Places a priority on programs that actually produce bilingual students, in keeping with the drive toward higher academic standards.

- Requires the Secretary of Education to "give priority to applications which provide for the development of bilingual proficiency for all participating students." This mandatory priority represents a major advancement in federal bilingual education policy, arguably the most important policy change since enactment of Title VII in 1968.

ESEA Reauthorization Becomes Law

The signing of the ESEA reauthorization bill culminated nearly three years of work by many members of the House and Senate and the entire education community. The most notable aspect of the process had to be the bipartisan spirit in which it was completed. This is especially significant in light of the elections of November 1994 and the new Republican majorities in Congress. Passage of ESEA proves that education and the well-being of our children are not, and must not be, partisan issues.

As for the future, I would hope that we could work for bilingual education in its truest sense. Students who speak only English should be provided with the opportunity to learn a second language, and newcomers and other language minority students should be welcomed and viewed as an asset for the expansion of the classrooms of our nation into global learning environments.

In some schools, this already is happening. It is happening in my district, at Evergreen Elementary School, the 1992 winner of the Bilingual Education Excellence Award. Dr. Eugene Garcia, the National Director of Bilingual Education, considers the school a "pioneer in promoting and demonstrating how children from very poor and language diverse backgrounds can thrive through access to excellent teachers and excellent curriculum."

I hope Evergreen can be a model for other schools across the nation. I look forward to being a part of that effort.

Footnotes

1. Lorraine M. McDonnell and Paul T. Hill, *Newcomers in American Schools: Meeting the Educational Needs of Immigrant Youth* (Santa Monica, Calif.: Rand, 1993).
2. Michael Fix and Wendy Zimmerman, *Educating Immigrant Children: Chapter 1 in the Changing City* (Washington, D.C.: Urban Institute Press, 1993).

Bilingual Education and the Future of America

By Congressman Toby Roth

Republican Toby Roth represents northeast Wisconsin's 8th Congressional District. He is a senior member of the House International Relations Committee and the House Banking and Financial Services Committee. Mr. Roth is the chairman of the House International Relations Subcommittee on Economic Policy and Trade. Mr. Roth also serves as co-vice chairman of the Congressional Sportsman's Caucus and as co-chairman of the Congressional Travel and Tourism Caucus.

Mr. Roth is a leading advocate of making English the official language of the United States. He is the founder and chairman of the bipartisan Congressional English Language Task Force.

Mr. Roth holds a bachelor's degree from Marquette University. Before serving in Congress, Mr. Roth established a successful real estate practice in Wisconsin. He served briefly in the Wisconsin Legislature, where he was voted Legislator of the Year in 1978.

On the Great Seal of the United States is inscribed our national motto, "E Pluribus Unum," which is Latin for, "From the Many, One." This profound phrase sums up the promise of America — a nation that welcomes people of all origins to join together in pursuit of common American ideals.

Indeed, as Americans we represent every language, every culture, every heritage on Earth. Yet we are one people, one nation. What is the essential element that mixes new immigrants into the melting pot of America? That allows them to compete and take hold of the American dream? One factor stands out above all else. Wherever they came from, whatever their native tongue, they adopted the English language.

Now, unfortunately, we are losing this cohesion, this unique

American blessing. One need only look at our schools to see this in dramatic fashion. In Chicago schools, 100 languages are spoken. In Denver schools, there are 89 languages in use. The list goes on — 80 languages in Los Angeles; 47 languages in Broward County, Florida; and 115 languages in New York City.

America is fast becoming a society divided by language; and with it we will inherit all the problems that stem from this development — ethnic strife, more discrimination, and entrenched poverty — the creation of an entire subculture that is unable to compete in the American economy.

The stakes could not be higher. The National Clearinghouse for Bilingual Education estimates that 40 million Americans will be non-English-language-proficient in just eight years. This represents about one-sixth of our population.

These Americans increasingly are isolated, and we are doing nothing to stop it. Theodore White adeptly summed up this tragedy when he said, "It is distasteful that a nation whose seal bears the inscription E Pluribus Unum should be asked to divide itself from the one nation into many tribes."

Americans believe the benefits of knowing our national language should be obvious to anyone. It is the world's and our nation's language of commerce, diplomacy, and opportunity. We must recognize this reality through a formal declaration that English is America's official language. In addition, we must re-examine the failed policies that have brought us to this precipice.

For most of our history, America gave the children of immigrants a precious gift — an education in the English language. As each new wave of immigrants arrived on these shores, the first task they wanted to complete was to make certain that they and their children had a chance to learn English, so they could get their piece of the American dream.

What are we doing to help these 40 million Americans who need help with their language skills? Instead of a first-rate education in English, our government now provides failed bilingual education programs. Let us take a closer look at these programs.

The last session of Congress continued the federal bilingual education mandate as part of the reauthorization of the Elementary and Secondary Education Act (ESEA). This action was taken despite the clear evidence that federal bilingual education programs are costly, with most of the burden falling on state and local governments. Most shocking, however, bilingual education programs were reauthorized despite the fact that they do not work.

The evidence has been in for some time. Transitional bilingual education is a dismal failure at what Congress has specifically asked it to accomplish: teaching students English. Even advocates of bilingual programs have been forced to admit that these programs do not work. Thomas P. Carter and Roberto D. Segura, in their book, *Mexican Americans in School: A Decade of Change,* confess:

> Governmental financial support (for bilingual education) will diminish rapidly as it becomes increasingly clear to legislators that the goals of improved Chicano academic achievement are not met.

The main argument for bilingual education at the inception of these programs during the years of the Great Society was that it would reduce the dropout rate among Hispanics. Have the programs succeeded? In 1972, the first time figures were compiled for Hispanic students, the dropout rate was 34.3%. In 1993, the figure was 37%.

Today, the search for proof that these programs actually help immigrant children learn English continues without success. Of course, proponents can point to an individual or two who will say that bilingual education helped him. But evidence of widespread success continues to elude advocates of these programs.

The most thorough study in this area was released in 1986 by Christine H. Rossell and J. Michael Ross. Rossell and Ross reviewed every study they could find on the subject from 1960 to 1984. Their aim was to find if bilingual education actually helped students learn English. The researchers looked at scientific journals, courtroom testimony, and the major studies of the subject to see if transitional bilingual education actually "worked." Their definition of "worked" took advocates of these programs at their word that the goal of such programs was to maximize "the highest English language achievement of which that student is capable." The two reviewed 79 studies and, as they bluntly put it, not a single study "has found transitional bilingual education to be superior to structured immersion" at teaching English.

Another comprehensive study found similar results. The American Institutes for Research (AIR) examination of bilingual education programs found that students in these programs actually were doing worse in English than their Hispanic counterparts who were not participating in such programs.

Despite this record of failure, advocates of bilingual education continue to demand that these programs be funded handsomely by state and federal governments. Yet these failures have human faces. Let me draw attention to just one. A mother in New York City, Gregoria

Jimenez, came to the attention of the press not too long ago because she was forced to hire a private tutor for her son. Why? Because after three years of bilingual education, her son could not read or write in any language.

Bilingual education is an abject failure at accomplishing the goal Congress set for it when it began authorization of the program: to teach children English quickly. It may very well be successful in accomplishing other goals, such as maintaining the native languages of the children enrolled in its programs. When children are taught in their native tongue and receive as little as 45 minutes a day of English language instruction, as is the case in many bilingual education programs, one can readily understand how this curriculum is actually better designed to maintain native languages and cultures than to teach children English.

But that is not what bilingual education was specifically intended to accomplish. Those who have other goals for these programs should say so and allow the programs to be judged on those merits. If the supporters of bilingual education want to use it as a way to maintain the language and culture of their ancestors at the expense of their children's future, let them say so up front. But it simply defies the evidence to say that bilingual education teaches students English better than other methods do.

The best-kept secret in this entire debate is that most immigrants, like most Americans, agree that teaching children in their native tongue is not the most effective way to improve children's English skills. Do these programs continue because parents support them? No. These programs continue despite parental opposition. One of the most moving statements on this subject was made by Ernesto Ortiz, a foreman on a south Texas ranch, who said: "My children learn Spanish in school so they can grow up to be busboys and waiters. I teach them English at home so they can grow up to be doctors and lawyers."

Thomas Sowell, in *Inside American Education,* cited numerous surveys proving that the great majority of Hispanic parents — more than three-fourths of Mexican-American parents and more than four-fifths of Cuban-American parents — are opposed to the teaching of Spanish in the schools at the expense of English.

In fact, all too often, the government requires parents to put their children in bilingual programs despite the parents' strenuous objections.

In one case, Charles Pacheco, an ex-Marine and native-born American, found his daughter placed in a Spanish-based bilingual education program strictly because her last name was Hispanic in origin.

Even after Mr. Pacheco informed the school that no one in his home spoke Spanish, his daughter was trapped in the bilingual class.

These feelings from parents are understandable. Consider the plight of the non-English speaker in America. The daily newspaper is irrelevant to him. The vast majority of the books in the public library are useless. Classified ads offering jobs and products might as well not exist. Filling a job application or writing an effective résumé is impossible.

The most tragic aspect of failed bilingual education programs is that they relegate their pupils to second-class economic status. Bilingual education, instead of easing the transition for new immigrants to America, actually imprisons its pupils below a glass ceiling of, at best, functional literacy and substandard English. An article in the *Washington Post* on this topic earned the headline, "No English, No Future."

New Americans understand as well as anybody the paramount importance of learning English in America. Bilga Abramova, a 35-year-old Russian refugee, understands. Bilga has entered a church lottery three times in an attempt to win one of 50 coveted spaces in a free, intensive English class offered by her local parish. Her pleas in Russian speak volumes about the plight of all too many immigrants: "I need to win," she said. "Without English, I cannot begin a new life."

When discussing the merits of bilingual education, we dare not lose sight of a fundamental truth: The future in America belongs in large part to those who read and write English well.

The entire world recognizes the importance of English. Ironically, our government is hindering Americans from achieving fluency in English while almost every other nation promotes the acquisition of the language. The Germans, the Japanese, and others are busy learning English. In the meantime, the government of the United States is denying American-born children the same opportunity; and the American taxpayers are paying for it.

These failed programs cost a good deal of money and impose onerous mandates on local schools. Direct government support for bilingual education programs totaled $215 million for this fiscal year. An estimate offered in 1990 during a congressional hearing on bilingual education suggested that this is only 20% of the total cost of these programs. That estimate turned out to be low.

According to a recent study by the American Legislative Exchange Council (ALEC), an association of state legislators, a total of $9,926,913,251 was spent in 1991-92 on special education services to limited-English-proficient (LEP) children. At least $5.5 billion, and perhaps as much as $8 billion, of this total was spent for bilingual education services.

Among these costs are the simple recruitment and hiring of qualified teachers. A school district without such teachers can lose all its education money from the federal government. At one point, Houston, Texas, nearly lost its federal money for failure to find enough Vietnamese-speaking teachers.

Some school districts will send recruiters to Spain, South America, or Puerto Rico to try to meet the requirements they face for Spanish-speaking teachers. Since until 1994 federal law did not require any teachers in these programs to be fluent in English, some school districts hired "bilingual" teachers who could speak little or no English.

It was estimated in 1985 that the federal bilingual education program had already cost American taxpayers more than $1.7 billion. This vast sum was spent with little to show for it. Billions of dollars later, there remains little evidence that these programs have accomplished what Congress asked them to do — assimilate immigrant children into American society. Instead, this money has been paid to keep too many children under a glass ceiling of substandard English and has relegated young Americans to a limited — instead of limitless — future.

If we allow these programs to continue, immigrants and their children will continue to be denied an effective knowledge of the English language. Without that knowledge, they will be left at the margins of our society, unable to fully pursue the American dream.

When new Americans find themselves without the basic opportunities other Americans have, our nation's unity and strength is threatened. Linguistic division will tear at the very fabric of the America.

It is time that this abuse of the taxpayers' money in the name of political correctness was eliminated. The evidence is clear. Bilingual education wastes billions of taxpayer dollars while failing to give students an adequate education in any language. Indeed, there is evidence to suggest that these programs actually inhibit the learning of English. We must eliminate these programs to ensure a bright future for our nation, and for Americans of every culture and heritage.

Dr. Henry Gradillas, the highly respected principal of the east Los Angeles High School shown in the film, *Stand and Deliver,* understands the fundamental problem with bilingual education. Dr. Gradillas objects to the emphasis placed on bilingual education because it diminishes a student's vision and future. In his words: "The bilingual proponents hate me because I disagree with almost everything they are trying to push on these kids. I don't want to teach students math in Spanish for the simple reason that the college entrance tests are not given in Spanish, neither are students allowed to fill out a job résumé in Spanish." Still quoting Dr. Gradillas: "When I voice these concerns, educators look at me like I am some kind of traitor. They seem to have already stereotyped me as being pro-bilingual just because I am Latino."

As Dr. Gradillas' commonsense approach shows, new immigrants who want to share the American dream and create a better future for their children are being defrauded by the American government. Their new country is endorsing programs that will keep their own children in poverty.

Bilingual education is simply indoctrination for a life in a linguistic ghetto. Thoughtful academics and new immigrants struggling to learn English both agree that bilingual education actually hinders the process by which new Americans adapt to our society and prosper. How many more generations of English-language illiterates will we allow bilingual education programs to produce before we demand changes?

English must be the language of our schools and our country. Not only do the American people in general agree on this matter — 97% of respondents to a *USA Today Weekend Magazine* poll indicated they wanted English to be declared our official language — but so do our nation's immigrants and language minorities.

If the parents of the children involved, prominent academic researchers, and hard-pressed taxpayers all oppose bilingual education, why should Congress continue to fund these programs? The billions we spend every year on failed bilingual education classes could pay for a good deal of instruction in English.

The Declaration of Official Language Act that I have proposed is an attempt to redirect our focus on English as our national language.

The bill is not, as some would have you believe, an attempt to eliminate the speaking of languages other than English from our country. In fact, the study of foreign languages should be encouraged. Multilingualism broadens an individual's horizons and is essential for the future competitiveness of our nation. But those skills are useless unless coupled with the ability to read and write the language of American opportunity: English. A solid foundation in English must be the first priority of anyone's education, whatever their heritage.

Neither is the bill an attempt to wipe out cultural diversity. Our nation is stronger because of the diverse heritage of its people. People should be encouraged to maintain the traditions of their families and forefathers. But the cultural elites would have us believe that practical instruction in English somehow robs new citizens of their cultural identity. This is absurd. Millions of new Americans have been integrated into American society without sacrificing an understanding and appreciation for their ethnic heritage.

What then does the Declaration of Official Language Act do? First and foremost, it designates English as the official language of the United States of America. In so doing, it states that English is the preferred language of communication among American citizens and that the federal government shall support and promote the use of English within its borders.

This legislation also would repeal federal programs that diminish or discourage the use of English among American citizens. We cannot afford to consign yet another generation to the economic prison created by poor English skills.

We must dismantle the multilingual bureaucracy that has taken root in the past three decades. My bill would eliminate the hundreds of millions of dollars spent on behalf of bilingual education, a program that certainly has outlived any reasonable time it had to prove its effectiveness.

We must act now to safeguard our country's unity. Declaring English our official language will help ensure that our country will continue to enjoy its harmony of cultures. In the past, America has been a shining example of how people from all corners of the world can live and work together in harmony. The world has marveled at how well the American melting pot has performed in fusing many peoples into one.

Today, however, America is in danger of losing its melting pot — and becoming a cauldron of division and separatism. Cultural and ethnic divisions, once swept away by the English language's power to unite, now persist and fester in our country.

Arthur M. Schlesinger Jr. in his book, *The Disuniting of America,* wrote of how: "a common language is a necessary bond of national cohesion in so heterogeneous a nation as America. . . . [I]nstitutionalized bilingualism remains another source of the fragmentation of America, another threat to the dream of 'one people'."

Bilingual education is very much a part of that threat. You see, bilingual education is a triumph of marketing over substance. "Bilingual," after all, literally means two languages. Yet bilingual education in practice is a program conducted almost entirely in a foreign language, with some English classes added on. The distinction is a vital one. No one is against students learning a second language. But the first language every child needs to learn to take his or her rightful place in American society is English.

Congress has stood firm against English-language illiteracy among Americans who understand only English. Why are we less concerned about English-language illiteracy among Americans who understand no English? This is misguided multiculturalism. It sacrifices the futures of generations of immigrants to the politically correct view that learning English is not important. These notions create the fiction that you can compete in this country — and take hold of the American dream — without learning English. This is fantasy.

It often is pointed out that the varied cultural backgrounds and experiences of Americans, when combined, make our country strong. Rightly so. But I ask you: Is not that strength diminished when diverse experiences cannot be communicated to others because of a lack of a common tongue? If our people cannot communicate, they cannot exchange ideas, values, or experiences. Bilingual education doubtlessly contributes to that breakdown in communication by erecting linguistic barriers between the diverse peoples that make up our great nation.

For all these reasons, we must eliminate bilingual education as we know it and again start teaching English to new Americans. Doing so will help ensure a bright future for our nation, and for Americans of every culture and heritage.

Impact Aid: Education's Bramble Bush

By Senator Claiborne Pell

Senator Claiborne Pell, a Democrat, first was elected senator from Rhode Island in 1960 and is the longest-serving senator in Rhode Island history. He holds influential Senate posts in the fields of human resources, education, arms control, health, employment, and arts and humanities.

Senator Pell has taken a leading role in eliminating the financial barriers to higher education. His legislation created the Basic Educational Opportunity Grants, which Congress named "Pell Grants" in 1980.

In 1965 Congress passed the Elementary and Secondary Education Act as an amendment to the then-popular Impact Aid program. Impact Aid, which compensates local school districts for the negative effects of a federal presence, today suffers from extraordinary complexity, narrowing political support, a perceived "pork barrel" nature, and, as a result, decreased funding. In fact, Impact Aid is probably the least endeared federal education program. It is a fate that need not be.

The underlying justification for Impact Aid is valid. On the average, school districts raise more than two-fifths of their funds from local revenue sources, mainly property taxes. Federal property, such as a military installation, Indian reservation, or public housing development, is not taxable. Moreover, often a federal presence not only reduces a local property tax base used to finance public schools but also brings many more children for an individual school district to educate. The schools are caught in a double-bind.

Prior to 1950, ad hoc federal support was provided from a variety of agencies to federally impacted school districts. The Johnson O'Malley

Act of 1934, for example, provided financial assistance to school districts with large numbers of Indian students. Taxes raised from federal Indian trust land were deemed inadequate to meet the costs associated with Indian students; therefore, federal payment was recognized as appropriate and necessary. In the Lanham Act of 1940, Congress acknowledged a similar responsibility to districts faced with large numbers of children whose parents were associated with the military. And because of the significant defense build-up as part of the World War II effort, federal payments became critical to many, many more school districts. By 1950, more than 10 federal agencies — ranging from the Atomic Energy Commission to the Department of Interior — had the authority to provide financial assistance to local school districts adversely impacted by a federal presence. In large part to reduce administrative duplication and provide for program consistency, Public Law 81-874, Impact Aid, and its sister Public Law 81-815, Impact Aid School Construction, were enacted.

Providing general aid for basic operating expenses to more than 2,000 individual school districts with more than 1.8 million students has always been a difficult and complex endeavor. There are districts that have no taxable property. There are districts that have great difficulty raising revenue from sales taxes, because more than half of all residents are associated with the military and can purchase tax-free goods at the local commissary. And there are districts that are unable to raise *any* income tax revenue from a large number of residents who, because they are employed by the armed services, are able to declare permanent residence, and hence tax status, *in another state.*

Over the years, efforts have been made to simplify and provide a degree of coherence to Impact Aid by treating similar school districts in large groups and identifying broad categories of students. I am afraid, however, that even the basic role that Impact Aid plays in financing local schools is far from simple.

Impact Aid payments are determined by a formula that, in essence, multiplies the number of federally connected children in a particular district by one-half of the relevant state or national average per-pupil expenditure. Since the federal responsibility for some children is considered to be greater than for others, certain children are weighted more in the Impact Aid formula. Children whose parents reside and also work on non-taxable federal property, called "a" children, are considered to represent a greater financial burden to local school districts than children whose parents work on non-taxable commercial property but reside on taxable private property. The latter are termed "b" children.

The multiplier most often used in the formula to determine federal payment is 50% of the relevant state or national per-pupil expenditure. At the time of the law's enactment, local communities, on average, contributed 50% of total general education financing. Since the federal presence may have the effect of restricting local communities in their ability to make that 50% contribution, it has long been considered a relatively good proxy for the federal responsibility to Impact Aid districts.

Further compounding the complexity of Impact Aid is the mind-numbing, idiosyncratic nature of so many of the nation's school districts and their particular relationship to the federal government. Many of these "special" districts deserve unique treatment, often in the form of additional federal aid. One such example is the Middletown Public School District in my home state of Rhode Island. Middletown, located near the Naval War College, is one of the finer public school districts in Rhode Island and is particularly well known for its special education program. Frequently, military personnel with disabled children request transfer to the Middletown area so that their children may benefit from Middletown's strong special education program. In the military's vernacular, it is known as a "compassionate-post assignment." Although Middletown welcomes these children, it does so at considerable expense. To educate special education children can be very costly — in the case of a single severely disabled child, as much as $100,000 a year. Imagine the financial strain on Middletown in years it is responsible for the education of five to 15 compassionate-post assignment children. I highlight Middletown's case not to appeal for empathy from federal policy makers, but to illustrate just one example of the many unique circumstances of the Impact Aid program that makes it a tangled web of policy considerations.

Despite its complexity, Impact Aid in the past has enjoyed broad bipartisan support from federal policy makers. In fact, funding for Impact Aid constituted more than 50% of the total federal education budget in the 1950s and steadily increased every year until 1969 to keep pace with the inflationary cost of education. Impact Aid was fully funded every year of its existence until 1969. Today, however, the annual appropriation is less than 40% of the full funding level. In the last 15 years, total Impact Aid funding has actually *decreased* by more than $100 million. Yet just to meet the inflationary cost of living increase over that same period of time, total funding would have had to double to $1.6 billion. In short, funding for Impact Aid, which is to meet the basic operating expenses of local school districts, has gone down, while the costs of those basic expenses have gone up.

Impact Aid was popular and well-funded until the 1970s largely because it met an unquestioned federal responsibility and was distributed to nearly every congressional district. However, in 1965 the winds of change set in with passage of both the Elementary and Secondary Education Act (ESEA) and the Higher Education Act (HEA). Federal education programs had a new emphasis linked to a clearly stated national need, such as poverty. From the 1970s on, strong competition for education dollars came from a series of programs, such as ESEA's Title I, Head Start, and the Pell Grant program. The fiscal demands of the last 15 years have made that competition an especially difficult battle in which Impact Aid has not fared well.

Policymaking attention has shifted to more politically attractive programs — such as Title I — and the Impact Aid program, with all its complexity, has had less attention and, most important, fewer advocates with a comprehensive knowledge of the program. The program also has been increasingly subject to amendments for "special" case districts by individual members of Congress eager to help meet the needs of a particular school district in their district or state. While special case districts may legitimately deserve unique treatment in the form of additional assistance, Congress rarely has examined special case amendments in a thorough and objective manner; the practice has been to accommodate the concerns of a particular member of Congress with too little regard for the coherence of the underlying Impact Aid program. As a result, less defensible special provisions for individual districts have been included in the law; and the program has become tainted with a "pork barrel" perception.

Further, as the law has become more complex, of more help to certain special districts, and of less help to a broad number of school districts, support for Impact Aid has waned. This situation was further exacerbated in the 1980s by a large cutback in eligibility and funding for "b" students and the districts in which they reside.

In the 103rd Congress, we began the reauthorization of Impact Aid with three key goals: 1) to simplify the program, 2) to direct a greater proportion of funding to needier districts, and 3) to eliminate the pork-barrel perception of Impact Aid. Those goals were conveyed by congressional staff to Administration officials and representatives of the National Association of Federally Impacted Schools (NAFIS) in repeated meetings prior to the beginning of the Congress.

The role of the Administration and NAFIS in the reauthorization is not to be understated. Because of Impact Aid's complexity and lack of political appeal, the Administration and NAFIS were, in effect, the only sounding boards outside of Congress for policy recommendations. There was no independent, foundation-funded commission interested in how Impact Aid policy might be improved. Even the degree of effort of Congress' own technical support arm, the Congressional Research Service, reflected members' lack of interest. Hence, the Administration and NAFIS by necessity were integrally involved in every aspect of the reauthorization.

To simplify the program and send funds to districts most adversely impacted by a federal presence, the Administration proposed to provide aid only for those children whose parents *reside* on non-taxable federal property *and also work* on non-taxable federal property, the so called "a" children. They suggested "b" children, whose parents work on non-taxable commercial property but reside on taxable land, be eliminated from the program. We accepted a portion of the Administration's proposal and eliminated nearly all civilian "b" students. Only in cases where there are especially high numbers or percentages of civilian "b" children in an individual district was eligibility retained.

The parents of civilian "b" children work for such federal entities as the Internal Revenue Service, Department of Energy, or United States Congress. Unlike military "b" students, their parents almost always pay sales taxes and income taxes. Unlike "b" students in low-rent housing, they generally do not come from poor or working-poor families. Such civilian "b" students often have only a marginally negative impact on school districts. Their elimination removed more than 200 school districts and 20,000 students from the Impact Aid program. It was a small blow on behalf of both simplicity and need in Impact Aid.

The major provision in the reauthorization for simplicity and greater concentration on districts most adversely impacted by a federal presence came with the elimination of a series of funding categories: Super "a"; Sub-super "a"; Regular "a"; Super "b"; and Regular "b." Under the old law and during years of insufficient funding (every year since 1969), districts with "a" students as more than 20% of their enrollment were considered "Super" and in need of a higher per-child payment. As one might expect, this added more complexity to an already complex program. Further, a problem arose in how districts were treated. For example, a district with 21% impaction was treated the same as a district with 90% impaction. Moreover, a district with 19% impaction received substantially less per child than a district with 21% impaction. In the reauthorization, we replaced the Super, Sub-super, and Regular system with one that better reflects the need for Impact Aid funding. As proposed by NAFIS, payment will now be the district's percentage of federally connected children combined with a measure of its budget dependence on Impact Aid.

Unfortunately, when it came to removing the less defensible special district or "pork" provisions in Impact Aid, we did not achieve our goal. Again, because of the complexity and narrow political appeal of Impact Aid, few members of Congress were willing to challenge less defensible special case provisions for individual districts. Either all special provisions had to be eliminated in the reauthorization, as the Administration suggested, or all had to be accepted. Unfortunately, we took the second option and backed away from differentiating the meritorious districts from those whose need is more questionable.

Despite our efforts in the reauthorization to make Impact Aid work better, the funding stream continues to flow against us. In the first appropriation bill following passage of the reauthorization, Impact Aid funding was cut by 10%, or $70 million.

It appears likely that Impact Aid will continue to be viewed in parochial terms and funding will continue to stagnate or decline in the face of rising education costs. It is unlikely that the complexity of the program will give way and that special district needs and advocacy will go away. The program needs a more widespread base and to be linked to a clearly determined national need. Perhaps that could be found if Impact Aid were an integral part of a larger initiative, such as school finance equity. Whatever, it will take dramatic change in the Impact Aid program or fiscal environment to gain greater financial support. Today, the former is more likely than the latter.

The 1994 Reauthorization of the Safe and Drug-Free Schools and Communities Act

By Senator Christopher J. Dodd

Senator Christopher J. Dodd, a Democrat, represents the state of Connecticut. He was first elected to the U.S. Senate in 1980. Previously, he served three terms in the House of Representatives as the representative from Connecticut's 2nd Congressional District.

Senator Dodd was the first Connecticut son to follow his father to the Senate. The fifth of six children of the late Senator Thomas J. Dodd and Grace Murphy Dodd, Senator Dodd also was the youngest person in Connecticut history to be elected to the U.S. Senate.

Senator Dodd earned his law degree from the University of Louisville School of Law in 1972 and practiced law in New London, Connecticut, until his election to Congress in 1974.

In the avalanche of federal education legislation during the 103rd Congress, often overlooked is the restructuring of the Safe and Drug-Free Schools and Communities Act, which was completed as part of the Improving America's Schools Act in October 1994. With a history of annual appropriations in the range of $500 million, this program ranks as one of the largest federal elementary and secondary education programs. For nearly a decade, it has offered flexible support to states and communities in their efforts to combat substance abuse among youth.

In 1994, the program was overhauled and expanded to include a new focus on school safety and youth violence. In addition, the state allocation of federal funds to local communities, groups, and schools was streamlined and updated to include, among other things, the consideration of need in the distribution of these critical federal dollars. New accountability measures were added to ensure that federal support would be used effectively to combat drug abuse and violence. The program also was affected by broad measures included in the Improving America's Schools Act that provide states and local communities with increased flexibility in the use of federal program funds.

While the Safe and Drug-Free Schools and Communities Program remains one of the largest federal efforts in this area, the problems that it addresses, particularly school safety, were on the front burner throughout the Congress. Action on the Safe and Drug-Free Schools program came very late in the session, but much of the groundwork for this initiative had been laid in the preceding months during consideration of other measures. Therefore, it is important to understand the changes made to this important program in the context of these other efforts.

Drug Abuse and Violence in Our Schools

Drug abuse and violence are widely regarded as two of the most serious problems that our schools face. The National Education Goals, as established by then-President George Bush and the nation's governors in 1989, include the goal that, "By the year 2000, all schools in America will be free of drugs and violence and offer a disciplined environment conducive to learning."

Yet in spite of good intentions, violence and drug abuse continue to plague our schools. The National Crime Survey reports that almost three million crimes occur on or near school grounds every year. The Centers for Disease Control and Prevention has reported that one in every five high school students carries a weapon to school. The picture of drug use is just as bleak. A recent study by the University of Michigan found that drug use had increased among all age groups. Over the past three years, experimentation with marijuana has doubled among eighth-graders, and daily marijuana use among high school seniors has risen by 50% in the last year.

Violence and drug abuse stand in the way of education. Children cannot learn, teachers cannot teach, and schools cannot work when they are engulfed by violence, drugs, and fear.

In addition to these immediate consequences, violence in and around our schools is eroding public confidence in our system of free public education. While the fight over private-school vouchers is an old one, it took a new twist in the 103rd Congress because of rising concerns about violence. The amendment offered in the Senate proposing a voucher demonstration program was directed not just at economically disadvantaged students but also at students who were enrolled in schools with a history of violence. The amendment was unsuccessful; but by promoting vouchers as an anti-violence measure, supporters were able to garner considerable support for it. Their success indicates the depth of concern about this issue and the appeal it has to both policy makers and parents.

School Safety Legislation

From the very first days of the 103rd Congress, school safety and youth violence topped the agenda. The Clinton Administration led the way with a budget request of $100 million for a Safe Schools initiative. In June 1993, I introduced this initiative in the Senate, and Congressman Major Owens introduced it in the House. This legislation established a discretionary grant program to assist schools in addressing serious violence problems through comprehensive violence prevention efforts, including peer counseling, conflict resolution, safe zones of passage to and from school, and the installation of metal detectors.

Following on the President's request for funding, the Appropriations Committee signaled its concern by taking the unusual step of providing this yet-to-be-authorized program with $20 million. This appropriation helped in the drive to pass the authorizing language, without which these dollars could not have been distributed to needy schools.

On the heels of this appropriation, the legislation was considered and, after several modest changes, unanimously approved by the Senate Labor and Human Resources Committee in November 1993. One change simply recognized the likely expansion of the Drug-Free Schools program to include school safety by adjusting the authorization of the Safe Schools program from five to two years, thus ensuring immediate help to schools without establishing duplicative programs.

The committee also modified the legislation to restrict the spending of Safe Schools funds on hardware-related items to 5%, in response to concerns about the effectiveness of metal detectors and other such measures when used exclusively to combat violence. With broad bipartisan support, the Safe Schools Act was adopted in the Senate as an amendment to the Goals 2000: Educate America Act and so was signed into law as a part of that larger measure.

Concerns about school safety extended beyond the education arena to crime legislation. The Violent Crime Control and Law Enforcement Act included several major new federal programs, including the Ounce of Prevention Council, the Community Schools Partnership Program, and others that seek to prevent violent and other criminal behavior among youth by offering them support and alternatives to violence.

Goals 2000 and Other Education Legislation

The passage of Goals 2000 in March 1994 truly set the stage for the Improving America's Schools Act, which includes the Safe and Drug-Free Schools and Communities Act. Perhaps most important, passage of Goals 2000 cleared the deck and provided members and staff with the resources and time to move on to the consideration of this massive legislation. This was particularly true in the Senate, where the one subcommittee with jurisdiction over all education programs had been weighed down with a substantial education agenda throughout the Congress.

Nearly every facet of federal education legislation was revisited at some point in the Congress. The Federal Direct Student Loan program was established early in the Congress to simplify student loans and lower costs to students and the government. Innovations in higher education continued with the enactment of the National and Community Service Trust Act, which provides thousands of Americans with the opportunity to serve their communities and gain new resources to pursue education and training. The School-to-Work Act offers states new assistance in designing education systems that are responsive to and coordinated with workforce needs. And, finally, there was the Goals 2000 Act.

Beyond freeing up resources, the passage of Goals 2000 set the policy framework for the Improving America's Schools Act and all of the programs it contained. In codifying the National Education Goals, the Goals 2000 legislation reordered federal education efforts to focus on high achievement for all students. With policy oriented toward results, flexibility and coordination among programs to ensure effective use of resources became an important goal for federal, as well local, policy makers.

The Reauthorization Proposal

These principles shaped the changes and the consideration of the reauthorization of the Safe and Drug-Free Schools and Communities Act. The Drug-Free Schools and Communities program was established in 1986 and has long enjoyed the support of federal, state, and local policy makers of both political parties. Since its authorization, this program has provided more than $3.6 billion for substance abuse prevention activities, including formula grants to the states and national program activities. As with nearly all major reauthorizations, the process began with a review of these activities and recommendations by the Secretary of Education on how to improve the program.

The major change recommended by the Administration was the expansion of the program's focus to include assistance for the prevention of violence in schools. Many of the new activities authorized were parallel to those in the Safe Schools program, fulfilling the promise of comprehensive assistance.

The department's proposal also modified the distribution of federal dollars at the state level to put more money in the hands of local schools. An adjustment was recommended in the allocation of state grant funds to the state education agency and the office of the governor from the 70%/30% split authorized in the 1988 amendments to an 80%/20% split. However, the governors were offered new flexibility in their use of these funds by the elimination of many set-asides that in the past had governed their use. The department also called for the state education agency to target 30% of their allocation to the neediest school districts.

Accountability measures were strengthened in the Secretary's recommendation. The governors and state and local education agencies were required to submit comprehensive plans for a drug and violence prevention program, identify goals for their program, and indicate how progress toward these goals will be measured. The Administration's bill also called for state and local councils to assist in the development of these plans. Finally, a national evaluation of the program was included in the recommendations in response to concerns about a lack of information on the effectiveness of these programs.

Action on Capitol Hill

The Administration's proposal was greeted warmly on the Hill. It was well thought out and responded to existing concerns about the program's effectiveness and lack of accountability measures. In addition, it linked the program to the timely issue of school safety, substantially broadening the base of support for this program. With such a strong start on the reauthorization, the process on the Hill was relatively uneventful, with limited involvement by members. However, some important changes came about; and, as with every reauthorization, new issues emerged.

There was strong support for the inclusion of safety in the program. But the Administration had proposed a structure of basic and advanced programs that limited the ability of schools to adopt such model approaches as conflict resolution and peer mediation until they had achieved a basic level of activity. It generally was felt that this limitation was counterproductive to the goal of reducing violence, because evidence suggested that some of these approaches offered the best chance of success. For this reason, both the House and Senate eliminated the bifurcated structure of basic and advanced programs.

The streamlining of the complicated formula that governed the distribution of funds also was widely supported. The House reinstated the provision that required the governor to allocate support for the D.A.R.E. program, which brings law enforcement personnel into classrooms across the country to discuss the dangers of drug abuse. Although the Senate did not include this reservation of funds, a more general set-aside for programs of this type was included in the final package. In addition, the final language also consolidated national program activities, including higher education programs, under one funding stream.

The application process was simplified further in congressional consideration. The role of state and local councils in the development of the plan was eliminated. There was a general concern that these councils would duplicate existing substance abuse councils in many states and that they added an unnecessary layer to this process. Language was included to reduce duplication of effort and ensure public involvement by clarifying that applications and plans for Safe and Drug-Free Schools and Communities funds should be fully coordinated with the planning requirements of Goals 2000.

One of few issues that nearly erupted among members involved the inclusion of support for character education in the Safe and Drug-Free Schools program. I offered an amendment, which was adopted unanimously, in the Senate Labor and Human Resources committee to include locally developed character education programs on the list of activities that could be supported under this program. Many communities across the country have adopted character education programs, focusing on such issues as self-discipline, respect, and personal and civic responsibility. Schools have found these programs to be successful in lowering the incidence of violent and disruptive behavior. The amendment was carefully structured to ensure that programs supported with federal funds were local programs developed by parents and others as a part of their efforts to reduce violence and drug abuse. In addition, Senator Domenici and I offered an amendment on the floor, which was also adopted without dissent, to include a small new program to support state and local partnerships in character education.

The House had a very different experience with character education in its consideration of the Improving America's Schools Act. An amendment offered in the Education and Labor Committee to establish a program to support character education was defeated in the wake of concerns about the appropriate federal role in this area. In the Senate, we learned much from the House's experience and were careful to offer support to character education programs with strong involvement at the local level. We also received assistance in our efforts through the formation of the nonpartisan Character Counts Coalition, which helped educate members about character education and its potential.

Ultimately, this strategy proved successful in the conference on this measure. House members were reassured about the intent of the amendment to the Safe and Drug-Free Schools program by additional language that strengthened the link between a character education program and a comprehensive violence and drug-use prevention program. The separate Domenici/Dodd character education partnership program was rolled into the larger Secretary's Fund for Innovation in Education program as a discretionary activity.

With these agreements in place, the only obstacle remaining was passage of the entire Improving America's Schools Act, which in the waning days of the Congress was hung up on several major issues, ranging from the distribution of Title I dollars to school prayer. However, with the passage of this legislation hanging in the balance, concerns about preserving critical federal education programs, like the Safe and Drug-Free Schools program, overrode the concerns about other issues; and the Improving America's Schools Act was passed.

PART IV
SOCIAL ISSUES

The Reauthorization of ESEA

By Gary L. Bauer

Gary L. Bauer is president of the Family Research Council, a lobbying group known for its nationwide efforts to address family issues. Mr. Bauer joined the organization in 1988.

Previously, Mr. Bauer served as assistant to President Reagan for policy development and directed the White House Office of Policy Development during the last two years of the Reagan Administration. From 1985 until his White House appointment in 1987, he served as Under Secretary in the U.S. Department of Education.

Mr. Bauer received his bachelor's degree from Georgetown College in Kentucky in 1968 and his law degree from Georgetown Law School in Washington, D.C., in 1973.

In the 1994 bill to reauthorize the Elementary and Secondary Education Act (ESEA) of 1965, the pro-family movement won several key battles. Unfortunately, we must consider the passage of ESEA a defeat because it will centralize education decision-making in Washington and seriously undermine parental authority.

The most significant victory was in the battle over credentialing home- and private-school teachers. The power of the state to regulate home and private schools through credentialing is the power to destroy them. It had to be resisted. H.R. 6, as the House version of the reauthorization bill was designated, contained a provision requiring states to ensure that all teachers were state-certified. As it stood, this language seemed to include private-school teachers and parents who educate their children at home. Mrs. Carolee Adams, a concerned home-schooling mother in New Jersey, called the congressional office of Representative Richard Armey (R-Tex.) to ask if this could be what the passage meant. Congressman Armey's office, able to find no other plausible interpretation of the language, agreed to propose an amendment to guarantee the independence of home-schoolers from certification requirements.

That was the snowball that started an avalanche of public opinion. Michael Farris, president of the Virginia-based Home School Legal Defense Association, quickly orchestrated an action plan that mobilized thousands of supporters. Over the next two weeks, congressional offices were immobilized by more than two million calls from constituents demanding an exemption from certification requirements for home-schoolers and private schools.

Here was an issue that had never been mentioned on the network television news, was never covered in the daily newspapers, and was never a debate topic on the weekend public affairs talk shows. In spite of the fact that the powerful National Education Association (NEA) has long demanded certification of home-schooling parents, the certification stipulations did not appear to be part of a coordinated effort. The congressman who had inserted the offending language, Representative George Miller (D-Calif.), swore it did not require home-schooling parents to be certified as teachers. But his refusal to remove it in committee added to the parents' mistrust.

Congressional offices are accustomed to receiving a lot of public comment on the eve of a big vote. But this was something else. The ESEA reauthorization bill was still several steps from final passage and, in any case, was not the kind of legislation that usually draws much public attention. This time, however, the language in question offended a group of constituents with a fierce sense of independence; they would not be easily appeased.

The message was simple; the urgency was clear. Within two weeks, hundreds of thousands of citizens contacted their congressional offices and demanded that their representatives protect the rights of home-schoolers by supporting the Armey amendment. Many congressional offices reported that they received more responses on this issue than they did on NAFTA, gays in the military, the budget battle, gun control, or any of the other hot controversies that came before the 103rd Congress.

Congress got the message. Practically unable to use their telephones for anything else because of the volume of calls on this issue, they brought the ESEA reauthorization bill to the floor to deal with this issue and voted nearly unanimously to eliminate the mandatory certification language. Representative Miller, who had inserted the certification language into the bill in committee, was stuck with the villain's role in this morality play. He cast the only vote in favor of his own provision. Armey's amendment was then overwhelmingly passed, with just a handful of Democrats opposing it, apparently for purely partisan reasons. The Armey amendment specifically guaranteed the independence of home-schooling families from federal interference.

Putting Congress on the spot to pass the Armey amendment was certainly a great victory for pro-family conservatives. No one could fail to be impressed by the huge number of people who were mobilized without any help from the "mainstream" media, the speed with which the message was disseminated, and the sheer volume of contacts with Congress. No doubt, it will be a long time before anyone in Congress attempts another frontal assault on home schooling.

But in the wider context of the entire ESEA reauthorization, which became law last fall, this pro-family victory seems almost to have been a misallocation of resources. It is a pity we could not raise the same level of awareness and commitment to oppose a bill that, at minimum, transfers more than $11 billion from family budgets to the ever-eager hands of the education establishment. Of even greater significance is the shift away from school autonomy and parental authority to a centralized education power in Washington.

The problem with this successful effort to defend parental rights was simply that it gave pro-family conservatives a false sense of security about the ESEA reauthorization as a whole. While home-school and private-school parents' rights were protected, public-school parents were further marginalized. The bill should not have been allowed to pass at all. Unless it is extensively revised by the 104th Congress, the pro-family movement will have to deal with its consequences for years to come.

If the same effort that went into passing the Armey amendment had gone into defeating the ESEA reauthorization bill as a whole, then a great victory might have been achieved against the odds. As it was, a very bad piece of legislation was passed, in part because the constituencies that should have opposed it did not bring the same level of intensity and scrutiny to the fight that they applied to the home- and private-school credentialing issue.

Outrageous as it was, the certification provision was only one of many flaws in the ESEA reauthorization bill. The real reason why this legislation should have been rejected is that it imposes a defective educational philosophy on the entire nation. The mistaken philosophy embodied in the ESEA reauthorization mirrors that of the Goals 2000 legislation. Together these laws form the legislative vehicle for an outcome-based education (OBE) philosophy. A brief overview of Goals

2000 and a more thorough discussion of the ESEA legislation will demonstrate their overlap.

Goals 2000 became law on 31 March 1994, nearly six months before the passage of the ESEA reauthorization. It is a much shorter piece of legislation that calls for systemic reform through the creation of a new national education framework. The result is that the federal education bureaucracy, the state education agency (or state school board), the local education agency (or local school board), and the individual schools are networked through a system of grants and subgrants.

Touted as completely voluntary, Goals 2000 offers grant money to any state that sets content, performance, and opportunity-to-learn standards and develops accompanying assessments. Opportunity-to-learn standards measure inputs such as facilities, textbooks, and practices to ensure that all students start with the same resources for learning. While gross disparities should be addressed, focusing on absolute equivalence of resources will detract from real education and be a target of litigation. States are free to develop their own standards and assessments, but the law provides grants for the development of national standards in each subject and for nationally certified assessments. The standards are repeatedly referred to as "voluntary national standards," but they could more appropriately be called "federal and coercive."

The real significance of Goals 2000 is in the network it creates, starting with the federal bureaucracy and moving down to the local schools. All education legislation, including the ESEA reauthorization, will be plugged into this network and disseminated to all levels, greatly increasing the federal influence on local schools.

When the $11 billion ESEA reauthorization passed with a reform agenda almost identical to that of Goals 2000, the "voluntary" nature of Goals 2000 became irrelevant. Links between the reauthorization of ESEA and Goals 2000 are clear, beginning with the countless mentions of Goals 2000 in the ESEA text. Furthermore, the grant application process is essentially the same in each.

In order to receive an ESEA grant, each state must submit a plan to the Secretary of Education. It must demonstrate that the state has "developed or adopted challenging content standards and challenging student performance standards," similar to the application requirements of Goals 2000. In fact, ESEA says that "[i]f a State has State content standards or State student performance standards developed under title III of the Goals 2000: Educate America Act and an aligned set of assessments for all students developed under such title. . . the State shall use such standards and assessments."

If a state has not adopted such standards, it must include in its plan a "strategy and schedule for developing State content standards and State student performance standards for elementary and secondary school children served under this part in subjects as determined by the States, but including at least mathematics and reading or language arts ... which standards shall include the same knowledge, skills and levels of performance expected of all children."

This is not an invitation or a suggestion, as in Goals 2000. Backed by the influence of $11 billion, it becomes a mandate. Any state that fails to develop content standards and student performance standards — the core of an outcome-based education plan — is ineligible to receive federal education funds under this Act, which is a major source of federal funds for schools.

The academic content standards must specify "what children are expected to know and be able to do," the same definition used in Goals 2000 and a formula that is virtually a mantra among the advocates of OBE. The standards must contain "coherent and rigorous content" and encourage the teaching of advanced skills. The student performance standards must be aligned with the state's content standards, and they must describe two levels of high performance, "proficient" and "advanced," as well as a third performance level, "partially proficient," to describe the progress of children in mastering the material in the state content standards. No one fails.

A new system of testing, linked to the "challenging" content standards, also must be developed in each state. One of the "findings" cited in the act is the claim that "low-level tests that are not aligned with schools' curricula [fail] to provide adequate information about what children know and can do and [encourage] curricula and instruction that focus on the low-level skills measured by such tests." In reality, the objection here is not to "easy" tests, but to tests of basic skills. Our nation's schools simply have not succeeded in helping many children understand the essential elements of mathematics and language. Critical thinking must have facts with which to work. One of the premises of OBE is that you can skip over the basics and move right into "higher-order" thinking.

This notion flies in the face of common sense and the experience of millions of educators and parents. Yet there is an impenetrable reluctance on the part of the education establishment to admit that the root of the deficiencies in higher-order skills is the lack of a foundation in the basics. It is difficult, for example, to expect a person to write graceful prose if he does not know the parts of speech.

States that do not have such assessments, at least in math and reading or language arts, must develop and test them within four years. If the state fails to develop academic content standards or assessments within the allotted time, it must accept those contained in another state plan that has been approved by the Secretary of Education. Again the "voluntary" clause in Goals 2000 is rendered a fallacy.

While crafters of the ESEA reauthorization are generous toward student failure — replacing that honest term with the more politically correct "partially proficient" — they show much less tolerance toward schools and school boards that cannot meet *their* standards for restructuring. ESEA proponents would like to create an artificial environment devoid of student failure by changing definitions and lowering standards; their actions toward rogue schools and school boards recognize that standards of success and failure do indeed exist in the real world.

A school that does not improve in accordance with its state's performance standards for two consecutive years may be singled out by the local education agency for "school improvement." The first suggested remedy is to review the school's plan "in the context of the opportunity-to-learn standards or strategies developed by such State under Goals 2000." Further "corrective actions" are more forceful in pushing the ESEA/Goals 2000 reform agenda on a school and infringing on local autonomy. Among the most troublesome are: "interagency collaborative agreements between the school and other public agencies to provide health, counseling, and other social services needed to remove barriers to learning; . . . decreasing decision-making authority at the school level; . . . implementing opportunity-to-learn standards or strategies developed by such State under the Goals 2000: Educate America Act." In the same way, a local school board may be "corrected" by the state board of education by "reconstruction of the school district personnel" or complete "abolition or restructuring of the local educational agency." These provisions make Goals 2000 a fraud. The amount of money behind ESEA compels states to accept the plan embodied in both laws. Thus compliance is hardly voluntary, and so-called local control is simply rhetoric.

The shift to outcome-based education entails extensive retraining of teachers, and so Title II of the reauthorization act sets up the "Dwight D. Eisenhower Professional Development Program." The retraining of teachers is an ambitious effort built entirely around the mandated state standards. The National Board for Professional Teaching Standards, established by the Goals 2000 legislation as a federally funded national certification board, will have a large role in this effort. Each state and local education agency must develop its own plan for professional development of teachers. One of the purposes that will be funded under these grants is a new affirmative action program to increase the number of minorities, disabled persons, and women teaching in the core academic subjects, especially in math and science.

One of the "findings" on which the legislation is based is that "all parents can contribute to their children's success by helping at home and becoming partners with teachers so that children can achieve high standards." References to parents as partners are frequent: "each school and local educational agency. . . shall educate teachers, pupil services personnel, principals and other staff. . . in how to reach out to, communicate with, and work with parents as equal partners." The spirit of the law runs counter to the historic doctrine of the Supreme Court, handed down in *Pierce* v. *Society of Sisters* in 1925, which stated, "The child is not the mere creature of the state."

Parents have primary responsibility for and authority over their children. This law seems to equate the importance of parents and school personnel in the lives of children. To say that they are "equal partners" is presumptuous on the part of the education establishment. School personnel should view theirs as a delegated authority; parents have an intrinsic authority over their children. Moreover, when it comes to education, the law's implication is that teachers have the real responsibility for the student and parents are sometimes invited to help out in the task. The school may have subject matter competence that parents do not possess; but as the definition of education becomes increasingly inclusive — sex education, values education, etc. — the school is no longer the education authority, for education has infringed on family territory.

An entire section of the law is devoted to parent participation in the Title I program. It provides that a local school board may receive funds only if it implements programs, activities, and procedures for the involvement of parents. However honorable these intentions might sound, developing a model of parent participation will inevitably place a ceiling on their input.

A school board's parent involvement policy must coordinate and integrate the Title I parental involvement strategies with those of other programs, including Head Start, Parents as Teachers, and preschool programs. These programs are objectionable because they contain features that detract from parental independence and family autonomy. For instance, the Parents as Teachers program entails home visits by a counselor beginning at the birth of a child.

The law also states that each participating school and district will assist parents in understanding the National Education Goals, the state's content standards, and the student performance standards and assessments. Parents also are to be helped to monitor their children's progress and to work with educators to improve performance. In other words, whether or not they endorse it, school officials are compelled to further the "voluntary" Goals 2000 agenda. They also must provide training and materials for parents to help them work with their children to improve performance. All these and many other programs and services must be provided for parents so that they can assume the role of auxiliary teacher for their children. But in every one of the provisions dealing with this subject, the parents are depicted in a subordinate role, helping out on a task that is the primary responsibility of the school and its personnel.

The ESEA reauthorization resembles a manual for parenting. It tells parents what to monitor at home, provides for home visits by professionals, and describes when and how parents should become involved in school activities. The law even makes provision for how parent complaints are to be handled. "If the schoolwide program plan. . . is not satisfactory to the parents of participating children," the school shall "submit any parent comments on the plan when the school makes the plan available to the local education agency." As for the district, "if the plan . . . is not satisfactory to the parents of participating children, the local education agency shall submit any parent comments with such plan when such local education agency submits the plan to the State." Parents' objections are simply kicked upstairs. Real authority to make decisions remains in the hands of school officials.

The exclusion of parents from any real exercise of power is glaringly evident in the school choice program authorized under Title I. Local education agencies are permitted to set up public school choice programs under which parents of eligible children would be able to select the public school their children will attend. On its face, any kind of choice program — even one limited, as is this one, to public schools receiving Title I funds in the same school district — empowers parents by giving them real authority. If parents are free to choose, if they have a right to remove their children from schools with which they are not satisfied and enroll them in schools they prefer, then school officials must be responsive to the concerns of parents.

But even the choice plan outlined in the ESEA reauthorization act denies parents any real power. It contains a provision that negates the very purpose of the school choice idea by requiring that "both the sending and receiving schools agree to the student transfer." That provision puts all the power right back into the hands of the bureaucrats. If a school principal has the power to veto the transfer of a student whose parents are dissatisfied with his school — in effect, to force a child to attend a school against the wishes of his parents — then parents have no real power. The incentive of schools to be responsive to parental concerns is gone, because the parents do not really have the ability to take their business elsewhere. A school choice program that puts all of the power in the hands of education administrators is worse than meaningless. It is a fraud.

However, one welcome exception arose that was contrary to the general tendency of the act to disenfranchise parents. In an amendment to the General Education Provisions Act, funds are denied to any state education agency that, either by policy or by practice, denies parents the right to inspect their own children's education records. While this may seem to be a minor matter, it is apparently the only instance in this entire 545-page act that grants to parents an enforceable right against education bureaucrats.

Among the "Programs of National Significance" authorized under Title X of the ESEA reauthorization is an experiment called the 21st Century Community Learning Center — an all-purpose social service delivery agency built around a public school. Only $20 million — the Washington equivalent of bus fare — is authorized for the establishment of these one-stop social service shopping centers, but that may be enough to lay the foundations for a new type of public agency. The 21st Century Schools are allowed to offer 14 different specified categories of services, including child care, nutrition and health programs, expanded library services, parenting education, employment counseling and training, literacy education, senior citizen programs, and other programs.

Nothing is wrong with using school buildings for nonacademic purposes. It has been a long-standing practice in all parts of the country, for example, to use school buildings as polling places on election day. In many suburban communities, school buildings are used for worship services by religious congregations that have not yet built a permanent structure of their own. Town meetings, community dances, blood drives, karate lessons, adult and nonschool sporting events, and exhibits of local art are among the many types of activity that commonly occur in public school buildings.

But there are good reasons to keep those nonacademic programs clearly separated from the primary business of the school. During the school day, any other activity occurring on the premises inevitably poses a risk of distracting students and staff from their work. There are few legitimate nonacademic activities that need to be conducted on school grounds during class hours.

In addition to the practical argument of interference with schooling, there is a philosophical argument to be made against the use of schools as brokers of government services. Such a practice tends toward a collectivism that is contrary to the spirit of our nation. If, from his earliest years, a child spends his days in a childcare center located in the school; if the child's immunizations and routine doctor visits all occur on the school premises; if the child takes two meals a day every day at school; if he attends summer programs at his school, and his parents attend parenting classes there; if, when he gets a little older, he finds his first job through the employment placement center based in the school; and if he spends his leisure time visiting the community library located in the school, has that school not functioned as his home? More important, by providing these services, has the state not functioned as his parent?

Coordinated Services authorized in Title XI marshals community social service resources. The federal contribution to this effort under Title XI is fairly modest. However, federal dollars are inevitably followed by federal control. Grants under this title are specified for hiring a service coordinator, purchasing basic operating equipment, and making minor renovations to school buildings in order to make them suitable for social service delivery, providing training to teachers and staff to explain their role in a coordinated services project, and improving communications among the participating entities. The social service projects themselves must already exist in the community. The coordinating service envisioned by Title XI organizes all of these services and makes them more easily available to students and their families at the school site.

This is obviously a convenience for the families of students at such schools, and it will undoubtedly increase the use of those services by the students and their families. On the other hand, without this assistance from the Department of Education, most of the social service agencies probably would not view school buildings as ideal locations for their programs. Furthermore, the heavy concentration of social services on a small number of school students and their families will tend to create a sense of dependency.

The Fund for the Improvement of Education authorizes a grab bag of education experiments, including environmental education, comprehensive health education, metric education, child abuse education and prevention, gender equity, character education, and "coordinated pupil services programs." These and many of the other possible activities supported through the fund are problematic for pro-family Americans. Environmental programs might well prove to be nothing but political propaganda disguised as a curriculum. The gender equity issue in schools is the outgrowth of the feminist movement; it results in an excessive focus on victimization and could threaten gender identity. Is a comprehensive health education program really about health, or is that a euphemism for consciousness-raising in sexual liberation? Will "coordinated pupil services programs" lead to de facto school-based clinics? Proponents of these clinics historically have used such vague terms as legal justification for establishing school-based clinics. These clinics are controversial because they distribute contraceptives and, when these measures fail, these clinics refer for abortions. Might a child abuse prevention program turn out to be a sustained attack on parents? And is character education a cover for the promotion of "tolerance" of alternative lifestyles that the majority of Americans consider deviant behavior?

Any one of those questions could touch off a major controversy in a community whose schools receive federal funds for these experimental "improvements." It is sufficient merely to list these in order to understand the risks. But that same Fund for the Improvement of Education offers grants for "eliminating ability-grouping practices and developing policies and programs that place all students on a college-preparatory path of study." This is another fundamental theme from OBE, and it illustrates the unbalanced thinking behind this act. On matters of gender equity, character education, and so forth, it is possible to lose sight of the impropriety of public schools subjecting students to experiments that may be ideologically tendentious.

Outcome-based education philosophers and the authors of the ESEA reauthorization and Goals 2000 legislation contend that all students can achieve the same level of subject mastery and should therefore be given open-ended time to do so. If we make the "outcome" of scoring a basket in basketball the standard of achievement, and keep each student in the class until all have achieved the standard, it is obvious that someone will hit on the idea of lowering the basket. This is what OBE advocates are doing. Through the elimination of meaningful student grades, through the de-emphasis of individual achievement (and the substitution of "cooperative learning"), OBE is profoundly anti-competition and anti-achievement. Such vague, behavioral outcomes have been denounced even by such moderates as former Virginia Governor Douglas Wilder and American Federation of Teachers President Albert Shanker. Shanker even dubbed them "outrageous outcomes."

If ability grouping is eliminated and every student is expected to achieve the desired "outcome," then those students who learn more easily will inevitably be held back while waiting for those who are slower to catch up. The only alternatives to holding back the more advanced students would be to establish different goals and outcomes based on ability (which brings us back to ability grouping), to do away with classes altogether and rely only on individualized instruction (which is not envisioned under this program), or to let the slower students fail (which contradicts the fundamental OBE dogma that every child can learn). That is why the elimination of ability grouping inevitably reduces the level of academic achievement. That is one horn of the OBE dilemma.

The other is the placement of all students in college preparatory classes. Some students are not prepared for college-level work. These students are not castoffs or less worthy of an appropriate education simply because they will not immediately going to college after high school. There are vital roles for them to perform in civic life and in a robust and free American economy. But if such students are forced into a situation for which they have no motivation, the result is likely to be frustration. Ironically, this sort of misguided effort to improve education could increase the dropout rate. Certainly, it will contribute to classroom disruptions.

Outcome-based education and its legislative vehicles, Goals 2000 and the ESEA reauthorization, are experiments. Students in public school, whose parents have not chosen to expose them to educational experimentation, should not be used as laboratory specimens for such purposes. Furthermore, the evidence that has been collected on the OBE experiment suggests that it is not very effective — all the more reason why public school students should not be subjected to it. Finally, parents all across the country have expressed their strenuous opposition to OBE, which is the best reason of all for not forcing this experiment on their children.

Education issues tend to be among the most hotly contested questions of public policy. The reason is obvious. Nothing touches home and family life so closely as education policy. No institution outside the home, with the exception of the church or synagogue, matters as much to family life. Providing their children with a good education is one of the gravest responsibilities of parents.

This explains why otherwise sober, mild-mannered, nonpolitical mothers and fathers can become raging tigers over a school-related controversy. Few acts are more tyrannical than to impose on a child an education agenda to which his parents object. Therefore, the power to make decisions about education should be kept as close to home as possible. It should rarely be allowed to go beyond the community and, as a rule, should not reside in distant, omnipotent Washington.

The Elementary and Secondary Education Act stands this principle on its head. It concentrates real power in Washington. It forces the states to adopt, in meticulous detail, an education agenda that is centrally determined and virtually identical from state to state. It punishes states and school districts that resist this top-down juggernaut of uniformity. And it strips parents of all rights except the right to have their complaint kicked up to the next higher link in the chain of command. Its approach to education is foolish and will make an already bad situation worse. An education system that takes power away from parents and puts it into the hands of the state is one that has become the enemy of its own people.

The Holy War on the "Unholy" Elementary and Secondary Education Act of 1994

By John H. Buchanan

Republican John H. Buchanan, Jr., served for 16 years as a Representative of Alabama in the U.S. Congress. He was a senior member of the House Committee on Education and Labor.

An ordained Southern Baptist minister, Mr. Buchanan has served churches in Virginia, Tennessee, Alabama, and the District of Columbia.

Mr. Buchanan also was the first chairman of People for the American Way, a position he held for nearly a decade. Currently, he is chairman of the Council for the Advancement of Citizenship. Mr. Buchanan gratefully acknowledges the contributions of his colleagues at People for the American Way Action Fund to this essay.

In 1994, the 103rd Congress passed two very popular and strongly supported education bills: the Goals 2000: Educate America Act and the Elementary and Secondary Education Act amendments, extending authorization for $11 billion in federal education funding over the next five years. Although little controversy arose over the actual substance of these bills, both were delayed by and seemed close to foundering on a series of amendments offered by forces hostile to public education and to the federal investment therein. These amendments focused on school prayer, homosexuality, private school vouchers, home schooling, and educational testing.

Proponents used a targeted grassroots campaign conducted by a coalition of religious, education, and civil liberties groups and a parliamentary strategy that included the development of alternative amendments. These actions, along with the help of House-Senate conference committee members, propelled these bills toward eventual enactment without the encumbrance of the ill-advised amendments. The focus in this essay is on these potentially harmful amendments and how and why they were offered.

A school prayer amendment authored by Senator Jesse Helms (R-N.C.) with help from Pat Robertson's American Center for Law and Justice, a right-wing litigation group specializing in school prayer and abortion cases, was offered first to the Goals 2000 legislation and subsequently to the Elementary and Secondary Education Act reauthorization bill. The amendment was strongly supported by the Christian Coalition, Concerned Women for America, James Dobson's Focus on the Family, and other members of that loose coalition, perhaps misleadingly referred to as the Religious Right.

The amendment would have cut off all federal funding to any state or local education agency in which anything was done to "effectively prevent" voluntary, constitutionally protected prayer in public schools. Since the courts themselves are in disagreement as to what is and what is not constitutionally protected, this draconian penalty would be exacted in a confused area of law and determined by the bureaucrats of the federal Department of Education in Washington, D.C.

The First Amendment not only protects free exercise of religious beliefs but also prohibits the establishment of a state religion. The amendment was one-sided; it would tilt educators toward erring on the side of violating the Establishment Clause in order not to risk losing federal funds. This interpretation, then, might lead to litigation from the left, just as too conservative an approach might lead to litigation from the right. One can easily envision a scenario in which badly needed funds paid by taxpayers to educate children would be drained away in lawyers' fees and court costs all around the country as a result of the litigation spawned by the Helms Amendment.

There is superficial popular support for "prayer in school," based on what appears to be significant misunderstanding of both the nature of prayer and what the law clearly already permits. As an ordained Southern Baptist minister for more than 40 years, I am well aware that a great deal of honest prayer takes place every day in public schools throughout the United States. Whenever a child who is a believer is confronted by a difficult test and lifts her or his heart toward Heaven and silently cries, "Help!" — that is prayer. When things have gone well, and the child in his or her heart says, "Thank you!" — that is prayer.

According to the New Testament, Jesus of Nazareth urged his followers to go into their closet to pray, that the God who hears in secret may reward them openly. He warned against praying to be seen of men. He also held up, as an example of how not to pray, a Pharisee loudly and pompously proclaiming a self-serving prayer in public. Perhaps pronouncements over a public address system constitute real prayer, but I sincerely doubt it.

Aside from the serious constitutional questions involved, there also is the pragmatic problem of how either a student or anyone else can come up with a prayer that speaks to a classroom or an entire school without offending or violating the conscience of any student. If the prayer is watered down to avoid offense, it becomes a trivialization of an important and serious religious exercise, but one that varies among faiths.

Our country is more than a melting pot; it is a mosaic of the world's peoples and cultures and faiths. In such a diverse and pluralistic society, it is positively good to learn more about the various faiths of American citizens in order to better understand and respect each other. But conducting actual religious exercises is the province of the home, the church, the mosque, or the synagogue, not the public school.

However, certain things are clearly permitted. In addition to silent prayer anywhere, anytime, students can say grace in the lunchroom before meals, so long as they are not disruptive. Under the Equal Access legislation previously passed by Congress, prayer and Bible study groups can meet in the school during noninstructional periods, as long as the school permits other groups, such as a French club or a Republican or Democratic club, to do likewise.

The Helms amendment was passed by the Senate in the Goals 2000 legislation but eliminated in the House-Senate conference on the bill. It was passed by the House as an amendment to ESEA but rejected by the Senate and eliminated in conference. Proponents of the amendment forced a total of nine votes on this issue. Congress did approve instead a more even-handed and reasonable amendment offered by Senator Nancy Kassebaum (R-Kans.) that denied federal funds to schools that "willfully violate a court order" regarding prayer in public schools.

I have indicated the role of the Religious Right in instigating and lobbying for the Helms amendment. The following letter from a coalition formed to oppose it gives some indication of both the rationale and the breadth of mainstream opposition. (Note that the Johnson-Duncan amendment was the House version of the Helms amendment.)

September 14, 1994

Dear Senator or Representative,

As educational organizations, religious and faith communities, and organizations devoted to religious and civil liberty, we write to urge that you oppose inclusion of the Johnson-Duncan school prayer amendment to H.R. 6 as part of the final version of the Elementary and Secondary Education Authorization Act ("ESEA"). The Johnson-Duncan amendment would terminate all Department of Education funding to any state or local educational agency which "has a policy of denying or which effectively prevents participation in, constitutionally protected prayer in public schools by individuals on a voluntary basis."

Together, we serve millions of students and parents, thousands of school administrators and school boards, teachers and child advocates, as well as millions of Americans of many religious faiths. We are firmly convinced, for the many reasons outlined below, that the Johnson-Duncan amendment would undermine local control of education, would needlessly interfere with the task of running our public schools, would undermine religious liberty, and should be rejected by the Conference Committee:

- The amendment places an unfair burden on school authorities by forcing them to navigate an exceedingly complex and sometimes contradictory area of constitutional law under penalty of forfeiting *all* federal funding.
- The amendment is draconian, withholding precious educational resources even for actions which unintentionally, indirectly or unforeseeably interfere with prayer in schools.
- The amendment would significantly expand federal bureaucratic intrusion into decisions by state and local educational officials.
- The amendment would invite widespread threats and litigation against school officials by activists seeking to force group prayer into the public schools.
- Although seemingly phrased in constitutionally neutral language, the amendment would actually encourage widespread violations of the First Amendment's Establishment Clause, and would thereby foster even more litigation against our schools.
- Finally, the Johnson-Duncan amendment is wholly unnecessary in light of the availability of ordinary legal remedies for violations of the constitutional right to pray and the very sparse record of judicial decisions finding violations of students' constitutional rights to pray in school.

For the sake of our schools, local control of education, and our Constitution, we urge you to reject the Johnson-Duncan amendment to H.R. 6.

American Association of School Administrators
American Federation of School Administrators, AFL-CIO
American Jewish Committee
American Jewish Congress
Americans for Religious Liberty
Americans United for Separation of Church and State
Anti-Defamation League
Baptist Joint Committee on Public Affairs
Central Conference of American Rabbis
Church of the Brethren, Washington Office
Council of Chief State School Officers
Council of the Great City Schools
The Episcopal Church
Friends Committee on National Legislation
General Conference of Seventh-day Adventists
National Association of Elementary School Principals
National Association of State Boards of Education
National Coalition for Public Education and Religious Liberty
National Council of Churches
National Council of Jewish Women
National Education Association
National Jewish Community Relations Advisory Council
National Jewish Democratic Council
National Ministries, American Baptist Churches USA
National P.T.A.
National School Boards Association
People for the American Way Action Fund
Presbyterian Church (USA), Washington Office
Union of American Hebrew Congregations
Unitarian Universalist Association of Congregations
United Church of Christ, Office of Church in Society
United Synagogues of Conservative Judaism

Another amendment offered to ESEA by Senator Helms and Senator Robert Smith (R-N.H.) and in the House by Representative Mel Hancock (R-Mo.) would have cut off funding to public schools for any program or activity having "the purpose or effect of encouraging or supporting homosexuality as a positive lifestyle alternative."

This amendment was strongly supported by the Lou Sheldon's Traditional Values Coalition, joined by the Christian Coalition, Concerned Women for America, the American Family Association, and the Family Research Council.

Had it been adopted, the amendment would have required extensive censorship by education officials, not only of curricular material and classroom discussions, but even of private counseling. For example, a suicidal young homosexual could be condemned, but not given any support by a school counselor or even referred to a professional psychologist who might help him or her.

Emissaries of the Traditional Values Coalition brought to the House of Representatives magazines containing photographs of nude women in provocative poses. They alleged that the magazines were examples of sex education materials used in public schools. No documentary evidence was provided to support this claim, and it is highly unlikely that any such material ever has been or ever will be used in a public school in this country.

Similarly, on the Senate Floor Senator Smith warned of similar sex education materials allegedly used in the beginning grades of school, but such materials were never intended — and doubtless were never used — in an elementary school curriculum.

The amendment passed the Senate by a vote of 63 to 36, with only two Senators speaking out against it. Once again, a broad coalition of education, religious, mental health, civil rights, and other groups set to work to defeat a damaging amendment; and the Helms-Smith-Hancock amendment was eliminated in conference.

In the House, Representative Jolene Unsoeld (D-Wash.) proposed amending the Hancock amendment to prohibit federal involvement in reviewing or censoring curricula and also to prevent legal actions by states or individuals to enforce the Hancock amendment. Lou Sheldon's group distributed flyers warning House members that a vote for Representative Unsoeld's amendment "will be scored in voter's guides as a vote to promote homosexuality and bisexuality in our nation's public schools with federal dollars!" Representative Unsoeld's amendment was passed.

Another lively but unsuccessful fight was conducted by the Religious Right for private school vouchers, which would drain funds away from public education and shunt them toward the sectarian schools that the Religious Right truly favors. This issue is being debated in a number of states and doubtless will be revisited on Capitol Hill.

Perhaps the most heat was generated by a nonissue. Representative George Miller (D-Calif.) offered an amendment requiring teachers in local school districts to be certified to teach the academic material to which they had been assigned. The amendment was clearly intended solely for public school teachers, not private, religious, or home-school teachers. Yet it generated something close to hysteria on the part of home-schooling advocates.

Led by such Religious Right advocates as Michael Farris of the Home School Legal Defense Association and Jay Sekulow of Pat Robertson's American Center for Law and Justice, thousands of followers poured calls and letters into the Congress, overwhelming the Capitol switchboard. Although the charges were totally groundless, the crisis was averted only when the House adopted an amendment offered by Representative Dick Armey (R-Tex.) restating what was in the Miller amendment in the first place — that it applied only to public school teachers. The home-schooling forces proclaimed this a great victory.

As a footnote, I cannot but wonder how even someone as bright and well-educated as Michael Farris can adequately educate a household of children while pursuing his active and busy career. I would not dare to try. How much less-equipped for this daunting task are many of his followers. In their zeal to protect their children from "secular humanism," "new-age religion," and "moral relativism," certain well-intentioned parents withdraw them from public schools and attempt an educational task for which they have little qualification. Sometimes theology and common sense come into direct conflict, and common sense and children emerge the losers.

To fully understand the adventures of ESEA in 1994, one must step back to 1979, when a group of secular far-right politicos in Washington, D.C., began to watch such televangelists as Jerry Falwell, Pat Robertson, and Jimmy Swaggart and to dream of the impact these preachers and their followers could make to forwarding the right-wing political agenda if they were enlisted in the cause. The group conceived the idea of the so-called Moral Majority and went down to Lynchburg, Virginia, to present it to Jerry Falwell, who liked it and agreed to be its leader. Soon a coalition of religious and secular right-wing organizations were joined in this 20th century crusade.

A principal part of this agenda was — and is — a general animosity toward public education and the "secular humanists" who are alleged to control it. The censoring of books and curricular materials and the attempted injection of sectarian religion into the public schools became twin prongs of this "holy" crusade.

In 1989, a guru of this movement, Paul Weyrich, challenged his fellows to organize at the grassroots level to make their forces truly effective. With the help of Pat Robertson's Christian Coalition, which had grown out of his unsuccessful presidential campaign, and others of like faith and order, this organization has taken place.

The Religious Right now has made significant inroads into the Republican Party and has won local elections to public office in a number of localities. Such organizations as the Christian Coalition and Citizens for Excellence in Education have specifically targeted school boards and conducted training sessions in a number of states aimed at control of education at the local level. The outcome of the 1994 elections virtually guarantees that issues dear to this coalition will be faced again at the national level. Even more surely, the battles will continue in states and local communities.

Earlier, I questioned the accuracy of designating as such the right-wing movement popularly referred to as the Religious Right. This is for two reasons. First, the so-called Religious Right is essentially a political coalition of individuals and organizations, secular and religious, who share a particular far-right ideology and are highly issue oriented. This coalition includes a percentage of evangelical Christians, mostly fundamentalists, some conservative Catholics, and a variety of others. Many adherents are religiously motivated and in their commitment and zeal comprise an impressive political force. However, the bottom line is their political activity and their growing mastery of the art and the science of politics.

Second, while adherents of such organizations as the former Moral Majority and the present lead group, called the Christian Coalition, persist in stating that they speak for God in American politics and on matters of public policy — and tend to think of themselves as "The Christians" in contrast to all others — this is simply untrue.

They represent one sliver of religious and political thought in a diverse and pluralistic society. Many Americans share some of their stated concerns, but a recent Peter Hart poll conducted for People for the American Way underlined that, when it comes down to specific issues, most Americans disagree with them. Those who disagree include a great many deeply religious church people who cannot equate Christianity with right-wing politics and, indeed, feel that their faith leads them in an entirely different and often opposite direction.

In education and in all of public life, we deeply need many more American citizens to awaken and take their rightful place as determiners of public policy. Noninvolvement and inaction make all of us vulnerable to militant and extremist forces set on driving us in directions we should not go.

Those who believe that the classics of literature should be banned, that sex education can be equated to teaching children how to have sex, that suicide-prevention classes constitute teaching young people how to commit suicide, and that drug-prevention programs teach the young how to take drugs, can have — and have had — their say in schools around the country. But those are not the voices or the policies that should prevail.

The most recent "holy" crusade of the Religious Right has been directed against outcome-based education (OBE). This is an education reform being considered or implemented in some form in a number of states. Its merits and demerits can and should be debated by educators and the body politic. However, OBE is hardly a creation of the devil and the epitome of evil, as the leaders of the Religious Right declaim.

Hysteria and paranoia are not good companions to rational analysis and reasoned debate. Neither are they likely ingredients of sound public policy. It is time, high time, past time, for the great mainstream majority of the American people, who reject extremism of the left, the right, or any other kind, to become informed and involved in the battle for freedom to learn and true excellence in education. Our children and youth are our nation's most precious assets. Our responsibility is to make sure they have every opportunity to grow to their full stature and become the most and best that they can be. Protecting and enhancing public education is a very good place to begin the fulfillment of this high mission.

Library
St. Joseph's College
Patchogue, N.Y. 11772